D0914973

VILLAGE AND SEAPORT

VILLAGE AND SEAPORT

Migration and Society in Eighteenth-Century Massachusetts

DOUGLAS LAMAR JONES

Published for Tufts University
by University Press of New England
Hanover and London, 1981

UNIVERSITY PRESS OF NEW ENGLAND
Brandeis University
Brown University
Clark University
Dartmouth College
University of New Hampshire
University of Rhode Island
Tufts University
University of Vermont

Publication of this volume has been aided by a grant from the NATIONAL ENDOWMENT FOR THE HUMANITIES.

Library of Congress Catalog Card Number 80–54469
International Standard Book Number 0–87451–200–X

Library of Congress Cataloging in Publication data will be found on the last printed page of this book.

For my mother and father

CONTENTS

MAPS AND PHOTOGRAPHS

FIGURES

TABLES

PREFACE

Unquestionably, migration is one of the central facts in the American experience. From Frederick Jackson Turner's "frontier" to the "other Bostonians" of Stephan Thernstrom's modern metropolis, historians have sought to understand the evolution of American culture in terms of its enormous population movements. Although much is known about the settlement of western lands and the movement to the nineteenth-century city, little is known about the patterns of mobility in colonial America. All too often our colonial past serves only as a backdrop for the migration experiences of modern Americans, somehow reaffirming that our colonial heritage symbolized a "golden era" of continuity and stability. From our modern vantage point, colonial Americans were motionless; only with the opening of the frontier, industrialization, and urbanization have Americans become more mobile.[1]

Yet as I studied the people of two eighteenth-century Massachusetts towns, the farming village of Wenham and the seaport of Beverly, these old truisms about the stability of the New England town seemed less persuasive. Migration in Beverly and Wenham was accepted and common, the rule and not the exception. Fluidity, not insularity, increasingly characterized these two towns as the eighteenth century progressed. But the more I examined the history of migration in colonial New England, the more I needed to understand the place of colonial migration within the context of American history. If migration began to contribute to a more fluid society in eighteenth-century New England, what does that fact mean for our understanding of both westward movement and urban population mobility in modern America?

Once I began to piece together the evidence, I concluded that the eighteenth-century New England experience represented the beginning of a transitional phase in the history of migration, anticipating the even more fluid and mobile American society of the nineteenth and twentieth centuries. Just as there was a demographic transition—a shift from high rates of fertility and mortality to lower ones—so too was there a migration transition in which rates of mobility changed over time, particularly from the eighteenth to the nineteenth centuries. The antecedents of this migration transition may be found in eighteenth-century Massachusetts, well before industrialization and the opening of the far western frontier. In eighteenth-century New England, some people moved to new settlements in New Hampshire and Maine while others sought out commercial towns such as Salem, Beverly, and Boston. All of them sought a new stability which ultimately meant a more fluid society.

This book is about the eighteenth-century origins of that migration transition, and it focuses on the people of a farming village, Wenham, and of a small seaport, Beverly. The evidence presented here centers on colonial Massachusetts, one of the largest and most populated of the American colonies and one whose people felt most directly the effects of both population growth and migration. But I have also tried to address the wider implications of migration within the American experience, knowing full well that the relationship between migration and society has constantly changed through the centuries.

Historians of colonial New England, however, have not agreed on the meaning of migration. The prevailing interpretation of colonial New England society portrays a shift from small, insular communities, those "Puritan villages" of the seventeenth century, to more individualistic, diverse, and even materialistic towns of the eighteenth century. At the center of this perspective is the idea that eighteenth-century Massachusetts was becoming an overcrowded society, one in which population growth, landlessness, and poverty forced struggling sons and daughters either out to the frontier or onto poor relief. Embedded in this view is the notion that migration disrupted the lives of the people of eighteenth-century Massachusetts and symbolized the decline of the New England town.[2]

As I studied the people of Beverly and Wenham, however, this viewpoint proved too pessimistic. Rather, this history of migration and community life reveals that many people in Beverly and Wenham used migration as an act of renewal, so that adaptation, not decline, best characterizes the origins of the migration transition in eighteenth-century Massachusetts. Indeed, some people in the farming village of Wenham *were* limited by their agricultural economy, but they began to seek security through migration. In Beverly, an expanding commercial economy as well as agricultural resources offered work to both native sons and newcomers. Whether we look at the "attitudes" of the people of Beverly and Wenham or at the "structure" of their lives, we come to the same conclusion: the people of the village of Wenham and the seaport of Beverly sought new ways to ensure social stability.[3]

Yet we also must recognize that some people were more able to reshape their lives than others. One of the central limitations of previous studies of migration in colonial New England has been the failure to identify the economic status of migrants as compared with that of permanent residents. The result has been that early New England towns have been portrayed as remarkably homogeneous. While early New Englanders were culturally homogeneous, this was not so as to their economic positions. In earlier essays, I described in detail "the strolling poor," people who moved about from town to town in eighteenth-century Massachusetts.[4] This present study, however, extends that work by not only investigating the poor transients but also delineating the social and economic characteristics of permanent residents and migrants in Beverly and Wenham. Only with the careful distinctions that I have drawn among the permanent residents, migrants, and transients can we fully assess the impact of migration and population growth on the people of eighteenth-century Massachusetts. This book helps us to understand who gained and lost in colonial New England, and why those who made advances did so as well as why others were less able to adapt. Even though not everyone in Beverly and Wenham responded to population growth and migration in the same way, their experiences resonate through the American past. Some successfully achieved a new stability for themselves and their children through migration, while others became part of a small but district floating population.

This study of migration and society in eighteenth-century Massachusetts represents the first full-length book on this important topic. When I first considered this subject, I was startled to discover that we had no study of migration in early New England and that what little we did know was confined to a few pages in several books and articles.[5] It seemed clear that historians of colonial America were interested in migration, but few had studied it with the thoroughness it required. I soon discovered why. Migration is usually an unrecorded act, and if I wanted to study the migration experiences of the people of New England, I realized that I had to turn to unconventional sources. My training as a colonial historian led me naturally to family reconstitution, a method of reconstructing the family histories of hundreds of anonymous men and women.[6] Thanks to rapidly developing techniques of research with local sources, like genealogies and vital records, it is now possible for historians to delve more deeply into topics such as the history of migration.

While family reconstitution provided me with a research tool, I also wanted to know how the migration experiences of colonial Americans compared with their modern counterparts. My training as a social historian led me to employ some of the methods of the social mobility studies of the American city. Since census records, which would have provided a consistent record of the people who lived in Beverly and Wenham over successive ten-year periods, do not exist for the colonial period, I decided to construct my own. Using provincial tax lists (as opposed to town tax lists, which were less standardized), I compiled lists of the residents of Beverly and Wenham for ten-year intervals between 1731 and 1771. By combining these lists with the evidence from the reconstitution of the families of the taxpayers, I created a profile of the people of each town for the middle decades of the eighteenth century. Altogether, I traced over 2,000 names from tax list to tax list, linking together the permanent residents, identifying the migrants, and gathering demographic, economic, and social data.[7]

I turned next to the computer to assist in processing the vast quantities of evidence I had accumulated on each person. Because the bulk of my evidence had to be derived from sources otherwise silent about the history of migration, this study is primarily a quantitative one. I can think of no other way of recovering the migration experiences of the hundreds of average men and women who are described in this study. But no special quantitative skills are required for reading this book, and I have kept many of the tables in the text despite the fact that they are analyzed within the narrative itself. In part, I have done this to support my substantive argument about the responses of the people of Beverly and Wenham to migration and population growth. But I also believe that it is important to convey the methodological dimensions of this study.

The comparative emphasis of this book is by conscious design. When I first read the histories of colonial Andover, Dedham, and Sudbury, I became curious to know if these towns were typical of colonial New England.[8] Gradually I came to realize that no one town could ever be "typical" or even "representative." I concluded that a comparative perspective had been missing from our approach to colonial New England society. To be sure, comparisons between old and New England have a strong tradition among historians of early America, but my own concern was the evolution of New England society in the years before the American Revolution, a society already established for over one hundred years since the Great Migration of the 1630s. In addition, we now have two fine studies of politics and community life in early New England, but both are based on a broad, aggregate analysis of almost all the towns in the eighteenth century.[9] I selected a comparative perspective that was sharp enough to reveal differences between the two towns yet still detailed enough to convey the richness of community life.

The village of Wenham and the seaport of Beverly provided a wide range of evidence, all within a manageable scope for detailed research. With both towns located in Essex, an old county that sprawls along the Massachusetts coastline to the north of Boston, they symbolized perfectly the farming and commercial economies of eastern Massachusetts during the eighteenth century. Shipping and commercial activities flourished in the ports of Essex County, while the inland towns survived on subsistence and commercial farming. Through our village and seaport, then, we will examine the differing responses to population growth and migration in a rural town and a growing seaport. While the people of eighteenth-century Beverly and Wenham were less migratory than Americans of the nineteenth and twentieth centuries, they were still surprisingly more mobile than we had previously thought. It is in the middle decades of the eighteenth century that we must begin to look for the origins of the migration transition in America.

The gestation period for this study has been a long one, and it has been nourished along the way by numerous people and institutions. My interest in migration in colonial New England first began while I was at Brandeis University, and it was there that the initial financial support for my research came. An Irving and Rose Crown Fellowship enabled me to complete the study in a preliminary form as a dissertation, while a grant from the National Science Foundation provided support for research and quantitative analysis. As I subsequently worked on the history of migration, I benefited from the generous assistance of the National Endowment for the Humanities, the Charles Warren Center for Studies in American History, and Tufts University. All of these institutions afforded me invaluable support in my research, writing, and final preparation of the manuscript. I remain particularly grateful for their continued support.

Equally important to me was the generous aid of numerous librarians, staff members, and public officials in historical libraries, court houses, and town and city halls throughout Massachusetts. In particular, I want to thank those who assisted me in my search for the people of Beverly and Wenham at the New England Historic Genealogical Society, the Essex Institute, the Beverly Historical Society, the Wenham Historical Association and Museum, Inc., the Town of Wenham, the City of Beverly, the Essex County Court House, and the Massachusetts Archives.

Several people participated at different stages of this project in collecting and analyzing the evidence. I am particularly indebted to Joseph Pleck for writing the computer program which I used in tabulating the patterns of geographic mobility. In addition, he provided invaluable advice on data analysis and computer programming. As I completed the study, Mary Hyde cheerfully agreed to do some last minute programming. While

I reconstituted the families of Beverly and Wenham myself, Bonnie R. Gray assisted in gathering some of the data. Margo Horn helped to code the occupational data on Beverly and Wenham. To these people, I am deeply appreciative.

I am indebted to friends and teachers alike for their comments and suggested revisions. Because I began this project in what seemed like uncharted waters, my colleagues in graduate school were especially helpful, composing, as one of them put it, "a community of little community scholars." To them I owe a special thanks: Linda Auwers, Nancy Cott, Bob Gross, Mike Hindus, Allan Kulikoff, and David Reed. Included in that group is Liz Pleck, who also read this manuscript with her usual perceptiveness. In addition, Maris Vinovskis offered valuable advice at the early stages of this project, while Elliot Brownlee and Steve Dubnoff made important suggestions for revision. From the time that I began to formulate the ideas for this study, Daniel Scott Smith of the University of Illinois, Chicago Circle, and the Newberry Library served as a resource person for the methods of family reconstitution in early New England materials. More important, his critical reading of the manuscript and our continued dialogue on early New England history have been of special significance to me. Both while I was at Brandeis University and subsequently, David Fischer read several versions of this manuscript, always responding with insight and energy to my ideas. In the same way, John Demos read and discussed the progress of this work over the years, always representing the highest standards of scholarship yet encouraging me to pursue my own ideas. I owe my greatest intellectual debt to John Demos and David Fischer; I know that this book is better as a result of their comments.

My wife, Virginia Drachman, understands the long gestation of this book better than anyone else. She has been a patient critic of my work, responding both to my ideas and draft chapters. But more than that, she is always there when it counts.

Newton, Massachusetts D L J

VILLAGE AND SEAPORT

CHAPTER I

ECONOMY AND SOCIETY

IN 1767, the General Court of Massachusetts requested that the selectmen of the small village of Wenham explain why they refused to help maintain a bridge in Danvers, a neighboring Essex County town. Such shared responsibilities had long been common, since the people of Essex County relied on these thoroughfares for moving their goods to market and for travel. Because only the people of Danvers profited—and very handsomely—from the use of the bridge as people carted wood and shipped timber to the mills and businesses of that town, the selectmen of Wenham refused to assume financial responsibility. In this minor dispute over the obligations of the maintenance of a bridge, the selectmen of Wenham clearly did not view their town as part of the commercial center of Essex County. They explicitly tried to impose the burdens of road and bridge maintenance on the market towns that benefited from trade. To these farmers from Wenham, main roads were a "Public Utility" which benefited those who needed to travel to market, particularly to towns like Salem and Marblehead, the "two Principal Seaports in this County."[1]

Yet only two years earlier, the selectmen of Beverly, a medium-sized seaport bordering Wenham, sought out the assistance of county officials to promote the maintenance of county roads. Specifically, the selectmen of Beverly wanted to improve travel from the villages just outside Beverly's borders —Wenham, Ipswich Hamlet, and Chebacco—in order to facilitate access to the market towns of Beverly and Salem. The selectmen of Beverly turned to the Essex County Court of General Sessions of the Peace, whose justices had legal responsibility over county roads, to ensure that all thoroughfares would be improved each year and that farmers would not place fences in the way of passersby.[2]

Despite the political differences that various town selectmen expressed over the maintenance of roads of Essex County, the very fact that there were roads linking farm towns like Wenham, Topsfield, Boxford, and Ipswich with the seaports of Salem, Marblehead, and Beverly suggests their interdependence. Precisely because of these economic relationships, both farm towns and seaports in the county survived during the eighteenth century.[3] Market towns like Salem and Beverly serviced the needs of the smaller, outlying farming towns, while the farming towns produced grain, cattle, cider, wood, and hay for sale in the market towns. But the seaport towns also depended on the farming towns for a wide range of goods and produce. The people of Beverly, for example, sought to improve one of the roads through Wenham and Topsfield because "great numbers of the Inhabitants of Beverly have Great Dependence Upon Topsfield [and] the town above it for Provision, firewood, Bark and faggot for the fish Stages [and] are liable to Suffer in the winter Season Especially for want of firewood. . . ."[4] The people of Beverly and other seaport towns relied on their economic exchanges with the farming towns for their very survival, not simply for their economic livelihood.

Slowly, but surely, Essex County towns like Marblehead, Gloucester, Newburyport, and Beverly combined with Salem to become a commercial region in eighteenth-century Massachusetts. These regional ports, competing with Boston, both serviced the inland towns and engaged in Atlantic trade. The result was that the economy of Essex County may best be understood precisely as the selectmen of Beverly and Wenham

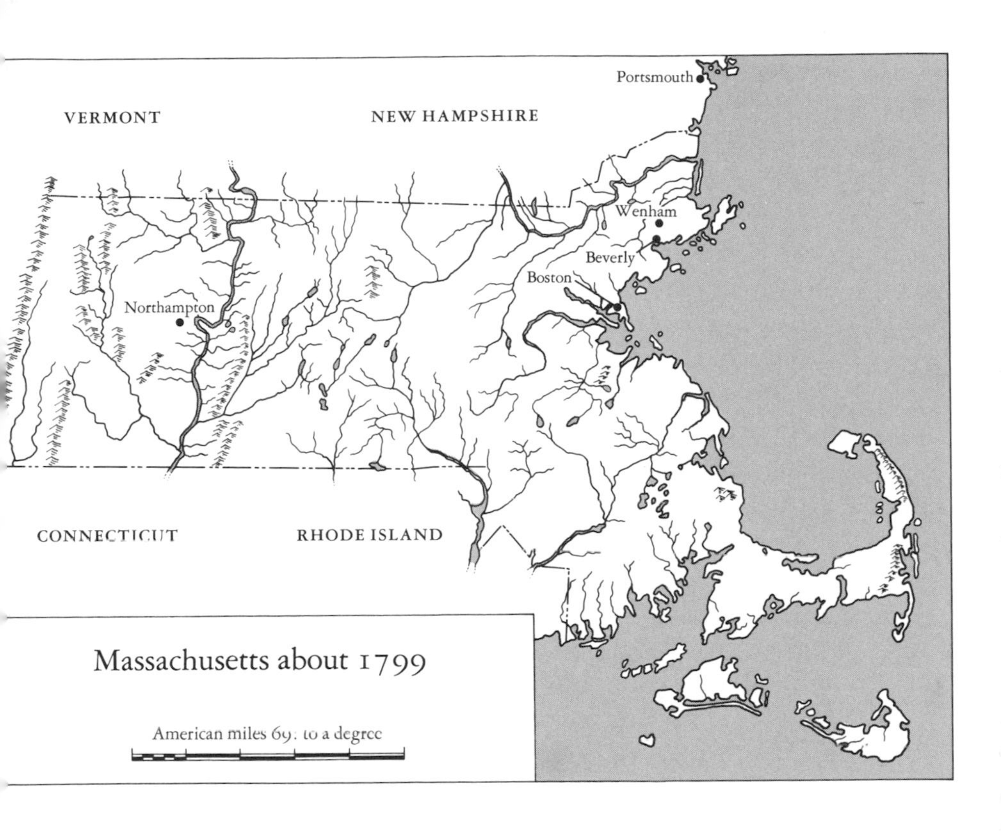

Massachusetts about 1799

viewed it: as divided between seaports and farm towns. With its mixed commercial and agricultural economy, Beverly's townspeople were more able to adapt to the dynamics of population growth than were the farmers of Wenham. While some historians have described inland, agricultural towns of eighteenth-century Massachusetts as "overcrowded" and facing a "world of scarcity," some towns, particularly the seaports, fared better than others. Although Beverly was not a large seaport like Boston or Salem, which could attract numerous people into their maritime and service occupations, it had a growing commercial life which made it better able to accommodate the pains of growth.[5]

THE REGIONAL ECONOMY OF ESSEX COUNTY

Economic specialization among the towns of Essex County was evident as nearly as the mid-seventeenth century. Some towns, Salem and Ipswich for example, served as trading centers since their settlement in the seventeenth century. Others, such as Marblehead, Gloucester, and Beverly, grew more slowly as the commercial economy of New England matured. But Newburyport, which separated from Newbury in 1764, almost immediately ranked as one of the largest ports of the county. From the middle of the seventeenth century to the end of the next century, the large and small seaports consistently ranked among the wealthiest towns of the county (see Table 1–1).

As the seaports grew in number, farming towns declined in their economic positions. The larger port towns accounted for more of the wealth of the county. In 1659, there were but four seaports in Essex County; a century later, there were seven. Towns such as Rowley and Salisbury, which had ranked close in economic terms to the seaports during the seventeenth century, declined during the eighteenth century. Some of the larger farming towns, like Andover and Newbury, held on to stable economic rankings, but the small farming towns, like Wenham and Topsfield, fell behind. These small, landlocked farming villages could not expand their boundaries and faced limited capacities for agricultural development.

The large and small seaports expanded their economic opportunities by beginning to compete with Boston for the fishing and maritime trade of New England. Boston's population and economy declined during the middle decades of the eighteenth century, in part, because of the emergence of the smaller port cities of Essex County.[6] While Salem was the largest of the Essex County ports, accounting for 790,000 tons of shipping in 1768, the smaller ports together contributed over 250,000 tons of shipping to the Atlantic trade. Taken together, the Essex County ports became a regional economy that competed with

TABLE 1–1. *Wealth Rankings of Essex County Towns, 1659–1790*

Towns	Wealth Rankings by Time Periods					
	1659	1670	1694	1740	1760	1790
Large seaports[a]						
Salem	2	2	1	1	3	1
Newburyport	—	—	—	—	—	2
Gloucester	8	10	10	6	5	8
Marblehead	10	7	4	4	4	3
Small seaports[a]						
Ipswich	1	1	2	2	2	4
Beverly	—	9	6	11	10	7
Danvers	—	—	—	—	8	10
Haverhill	—	—	9	8	11	9
Farming towns						
Newbury	3	3	3	3	1	5
Andover	7	8	8	5	6	6
Lynn	4	4	5	7	7	14
Amesbury	—	—	16	10	13	15
Rowley	5	5	7	12	9	11
Salisbury	6	6	13	9	12	12
Bradford	—	—	15	14	14	13
Methuen	—	—	—	19	17	16
Boxford	—	—	14	13	15	17
Manchester	12	13	17	17	20	22
Topsfield	9	11	11	15	16	18
Middleton	—	—	—	18	18	19
Wenham	11	12	12	16	19	20
Lynnfield	—	—	—	—	—	21
Total towns	12	13	17	19	20	22

NOTE: The wealth rankings of Essex County towns are taken from "County Credits . . . 1658/9," *Massachusetts Archives,* v. 100, 69; "The Country is Debtors . . . 1669/70," ibid., 148; "Act for Tax Levy in 1694," ibid., 507; Court of General Sessions of the Peace, 1726–1744, Essex County, Clerk of Court, Salem, Massachusetts, 1740 at p. 663; Court of General Sessions of the Peace, 1749–1760, Essex County, 1760 at p. 311; Joseph B. Felt, "Statistics of Taxation in Massachusetts, including Valuation and Property," *Collections of the American Statistical Association,* I, Part III (Boston, 1847), 558–59, for 1790 listings.

[a] Seaports have been defined as those towns which were assessed for commercial wharf footage in the valuation of 1768; see "Valuation of 1768," *Massachusetts Archives,* v. 130, 91–111.

the Boston merchants and markets. Beverly, for example, was situated within the shadow of Salem and benefited from the growth of this major port. By the eve of the Revolution, large and small seaports dominated the jagged coastline of Essex County, with each port maintaining ties to the inland villages and to the Atlantic economy.[7]

This division between farm towns and seaports typified economic activities in eighteenth-century Essex County. Farming towns like Andover, Rowley, and Wenham produced grains, cattle, and timber for sale in the surrounding market towns, usually the seaports, or occasionally to local traders. Meanwhile, the seaports provided services for the farm towns—mills, distilleries, warehouses, workhouses, and shipping facilities.[8] Salem dominated this regional economy because of its central location, large size, and accessible harbor, but other ports emerged as well.

The most distinctive economic characteristic of the large seaports of Essex County was their extensive commercial wharf space. In absolute terms, Salem's was the largest, with 51,131 feet of commercial wharf, and Newburyport ranked a close second. Together, the large ports provided merchants and traders with over 135,000 feet of wharf space, an important inducement for Atlantic traders as well as the source of jobs for the people of Essex County towns. For these large ports, maritime activities became one of the major sectors of the economy. With the limited technological and organizational development of businesses of the eighteenth century, only Salem and Newburyport had economies that supported more than a few mills, distilleries, iron works, and warehouses (see Table 1–2).

The four largest seaports produced much less grain and cattle than did either the small seaports or the farm towns. It was the farm towns, and to a lesser extent the small seaports, that were responsible for raising grain both for the people of Essex County and for export. Salem, for example, produced

TABLE 1–2. *Selected Economic Characteristics of Essex County Towns in 1768, Per Capita*

Towns	Businesses[a]	Pastures	Bushels of Grain	Draft Animals[b]	Consumption Animals[c]	Wharf Footage
Large seaports[d]						
Salem	0.18	0.53	2.6	0.14	0.25	41.8
Newburyport	0.19	0.12	3.7	0.15	0.43	63.7
Marblehead	0.09	0.27	2.1	0.14	0.21	9.5
Gloucester	0.10	1.29	4.7	0.34	1.89	25.1
Small seaports						
Beverly	0.10	2.24	21.9	0.63	3.82	10.1
Danvers	0.14	2.58	30.8	1.07	4.85	6.8
Ipswich	0.08	3.86	38.2	1.08	7.06	1.2
Haverhill	0.14	2.06	27.3	0.87	4.14	6.6
Farming towns						
Andover	0.06	3.92	49.8	1.64	6.66	—
Amesbury	0.07	2.15	23.9	0.69	3.43	—
Boxford	0.05	4.32	34.7	1.81	8.66	—
Bradford	0.15	3.17	41.5	1.02	6.35	—
Lynn	0.07	2.04	26.3	0.82	4.44	—
Manchester	0.09	1.59	14.2	0.41	1.86	—
Methuen	0.07	2.28	43.1	1.47	7.31	—
Middleton	0.15	3.74	32.5	1.51	7.37	—
Newbury	0.11	4.55	42.9	1.15	5.97	—
Rowley	0.06	4.34	40.6	1.38	6.92	—
Salisbury	0.09	2.48	20.2	0.72	4.70	—
Topsfield	0.08	3.44	41.7	1.62	8.28	—
Wenham	0.12	2.90	35.3	0.61	6.67	—
Median						
Large ports	0.14	0.40	3.2	0.15	0.34	33.4
Small ports	0.12	2.41	29.1	0.97	4.50	6.7
Farming towns	0.08	3.17	35.5	1.15	6.66	—

SOURCE: "Valuations of 1768," *Massachusetts Archives,* v. 130, 91–111.

NOTE: As used in this table, per capita figures have been defined as the number of taxable males (polls) per town.

[a] Businesses include all workhouses, warehouses, distilleries, mills, and ironworks.

[b] Draft animals are horses and oxen.

[c] Consumption animals are cows, sheep, and swine.

[d] Large seaports include those that had the most assessed, commercial wharf footage. Towns that also abutted the coastline and had some shipping did not meet the criterion of commercial wharf footage assessed as property.

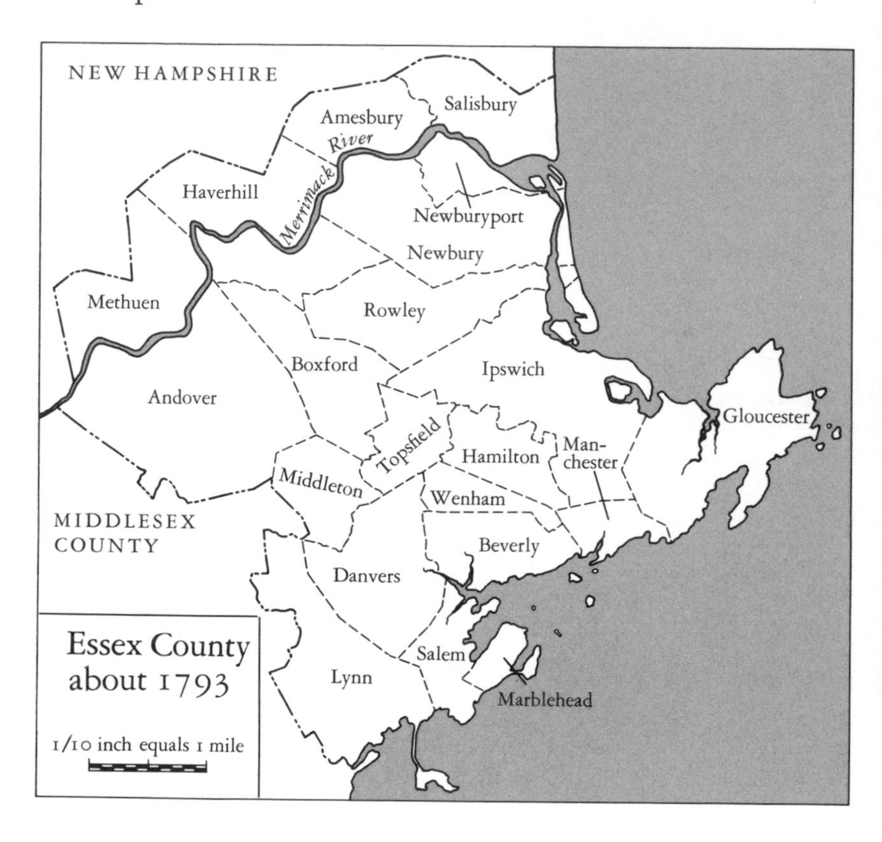

only about two-and-one-half bushels of grain for every taxable male, while Andover produced almost fifty bushels. Contemporaries estimated that thirty bushels of grain were needed to feed a family and its cattle for one year.[9] Salem and Andover represent the extremes; the median level of production of grain was about thirty-five bushels for the farm towns, twenty-nine bushels for the small seaports, and only three bushels for the large seaports. If thirty bushels of grain were needed to sustain a family for one year, then it appears that some of the farming towns, like Andover, Newbury, and Rowley, were more market-oriented than the smaller farm towns. Only those towns with a substantial surplus could actually engage continually in selling grain, no matter how badly the grain was needed by the large ports.

The wealthy farming towns were able to put more land to pasturage. Newbury was the town with the most substantial land at pasturage, with just over four-and-one-half pastures per taxable male. Manchester was at the low end, with only one-and-one-half pastures per taxable male. Unlike the large seaports, which had very few pastures per taxable male, the small seaports more closely resembled the agricultural towns. Beverly, Danvers, Ipswich, and Haverhill all put substantial amounts of land into both pasturage and raising grain.

The absence of draft animals such as horses and oxen in the large seaports accentuated the differences between the ports and the farming towns. Without substantial pasture and farming lands, the large ports had less need for these animals. It was in the labor-intensive farming areas where they were more numerous.

Yet the large ports depended on the smaller ports and farming towns for the cattle, sheep, and swine they consumed. The large ports did not raise even an average of one such animal per taxable male, while the small ports and the farming towns raised median numbers of cattle of 4.50 and 6.66, respectively. Available land was the critical factor in raising sheep and cattle, and the farming towns handled this specialized task.

The patterns of land use in mid-eighteenth-century Essex County reinforced the interdependence of the farmtowns and the seaports.[10] Cattle, sheep, and swine were particularly important in Essex County, with over one-half of the improved acreage of the county devoted to pasture lands. Another one-third of the improved land was for raising hay. The remaining improved land was for tillage and orchards. Of all of the counties of Massachusetts in 1751, Essex had the highest number of acres of pasture land; clearly, cattle, sheep, and swine were a central part of the agricultural economy of the inland towns. But the production of grain was less important for the farmers of Essex County. The county ranked eighth out of eleven counties in the number of acres under tillage. Although Essex County had the highest number of taxable males in Massachusetts in 1751, it still ranked almost at the bottom in absolute number of acres tilled because of its rocky soil and the commercial economy of its seaports. In neighboring Middlesex County, for example, there were over three acres of tillage land for every taxable male, while in Essex, there was less than one acre of tillage. Patterns of land use helped to shape and to reinforce the distinctions between farm towns and seaports in eighteenth-century Essex County. The large ports, commercial in their orientation, both serviced and depended on the agricultural sector of the Essex County economy. The small ports fell within the commercial and agricultural sectors, mixing the functions of each, while the farm towns relied on the markets of the port towns. (See Plate 1–1.)

THE ECONOMIC STRUCTURE OF BEVERLY AND WENHAM

Although neither Beverly nor Wenham was typical or representative of all of the other towns of Essex County, Beverly symbolized the emerging commercial economy and Wenham symbolized the small farming village. Beverly's population, for example, numbered just over 2,000 persons in 1765, only one-half the size of Salem. But with its twenty square miles of land and its natural harbor, Beverly enjoyed the benefits of a commercial and agricultural economy. By contrast, Wenham was the smallest town of the county, numbering only 531 people who spread across its seven square miles of land. Wenham never changed its boundaries from the date of its founding (1643)—an unusual stability for a New England town—while Beverly, founded in 1668, annexed a portion of Salem in 1753. Both towns underwent the same process of population growth

IT is agreed between the Master, Seamen, and Mariners of the *Brigantine Nancy of Newbury port*
John Moulton Master, now bound for the Port of *Newbury port*

THAT in consideration of the Monthly or other Wages, against each respective Seaman and Mariner's Name hereunto set, they severally shall and will perform the above-mentioned voyage; and the said Master doth hereby agree with, and hire the said Seamen and Mariners, for the said voyage, at such monthly wages, to be paid pursuant to the laws of *the United States of America* ——And they, the said Seamen and Mariners, do hereby promise and oblige themselves to do their duty and obey the lawful commands of their Officers on board of the said ship, or on board the boats thereunto belonging, as becomes good and faithful Seamen and Mariners; and at all places where the said ship shall put in, or anchor at, during the said voyage, to do their best endeavours for the preservation of the said ship and cargo, and do not neglect or refuse doing their duty by Day or by Night, nor go out of the said ship on board any other vessel, or on shore, under any pretence whatsoever, without leave first obtained of the Captain or commanding officer on board: That in default thereof, they will not only be liable to the penalties mentioned in an act of the Congress of the United States of America, passed the 20th day of July, 1790, entitled, "An act for the government and regulation of Seamen in the Merchant's service," but will further, in case they should on any account whatsoever, leave or desert the said ship without the Master's consent, until the above said voyage be ended, and the ship discharged of her loading, be liable to forfeit and lose what wages may at such time of their desertion be due to them, together with every the goods, chattels, &c. on board, renouncing by these presents, all right, title, demand, and pretention thereunto forever, for them, their Heirs, Executors and Administrators. And be it further agreed by both parties that eight and forty hours absence, without leave, shall be deemed a total desertion, and render such seamen and Mariners liable to the penalties above-mentioned. That each and every lawful command which the said Master shall think necessary hereafter to issue for the effectual government of the said vessel, suppressing immorality and vice of all kinds, be strictly complied with, under the penalty of the person or persons disobeying, forfeiting his or their whole wages, or hire, together with every thing belonging to him or them on board the said vessel. And it is further agreed on, that no Officer or Seaman belonging to the said ship, shall demand or be entitled to his wages, or any part thereof, until the arrival of the said ship at the above-mentioned port of discharge in *Newbury Port*

THAT each Seaman and Mariner, who shall well and truly perform the above-mentioned voyage (provided always that there be no plunderage, embezzlement or other unlawful acts, committed on the said vessel's cargo or stores) be entitled to the wages or hire that may become due to him, pursuant to this agreement. That for the due performance of each and every of the above-mentioned articles, agreement, and acknowledgment of their being voluntarily, and without compulsion, or any clandestine means being used, agreed to and signed by us. IN TESTIMONY WHEREOF, we have each and every of us under affixed our Hands, the month and day against our names affixed, and in the year of our Lord one thousand *seven* hundred and *Ninety seven*

Place and Time of Entry.		Mens Names.	Age	Quality.	Wages per Month.	Wages advanced.	Birth Place.	Residence.	Witnesses to each signing.
1797 Bremen June	*29th*	*John Moulton*	*29*	*Master*	*$ 80*		*Wenham*	*Wenham*	*Walter Conner*
Do	*Do*	*Nathl Boardman*	*23*	*Mate*	*$ 30*		*Exeter*	*Exeter*	
Do	*Do*	*John Kimby*	*23*	*Seaman*	*$ 20*		*Ipswich*	*Wenham*	
Do	*Do*	*Robert his + mark Bray*	*20*	*Seaman*	*$ 20*		*Marblehead*	*Marblehead*	*Shubael Snow*
							Baltimore	*Baltimore*	
Do	*Do*	*Gabriel his + mark Reed*	*21*	*Seaman*	*$ 20*				
Do	*Do*	*Richard Cook*	*24*	*Seaman*	*$ 28*		*Boston*	*Boston*	
Do	*Do*	*John Plummer*	*14*	*Boy*	*$ 8*		*Wenham*	*Beverly*	
July	*13th*	*Sm: Lingren*	*32*	*Seaman*	*$ 10.*		*Gottenburg*	*Gottenburg*	

This is to certify that the above wrote here above are signed from the Capt. John Moulton & six of his Shipscrew mentioned here, according here Declaration, which I do testify according my Office Bremen in the [illegible] *Month June 1797*
Pfeiffer, Receiver in the [illegible] *Bremen in the Dukedom of* [illegible]

John Moulton, Master of the Brig Nancy, American property, made Oath before me, that the above Seaman are all duly registered with him, and are Citizens of the United States of America. Witness my Hand and Seal of Office, Bremen this tenth day of July, One Thousand Seven Hundred and Ninety Seven
Friedr. Jacob Wichelhausen
Consul of the United States of Am

PLATE 1–1. Letter of agreement between John Moulton, Master, and the seamen and mariners of the Brigantine *Nancy* of Newburyport, 1797. Courtesy Wenham Historical Association and Museum, Inc., Wenham, Massachusetts.

familiar to other towns in eastern Massachusetts. Beverly, with its mixed commercial and agricultural economy, was more able to capitalize on population growth and migration than Wenham was with its farming economy.

As the eighteenth century progressed, both Beverly and Wenham began to rely increasingly on the taxation of property rather than on that of persons. Yet this shift to the taxation of property occurred differently in each town. In Beverly, commercial property, by 1790, accounted for the highest component of total taxation, while in Wenham, real property comprised the bulk of taxable property (see Fig. 1–1). In 1741, the poll tax accounted for 52 percent of the total taxes paid in Beverly, and 48 percent in Wenham. By 1790, poll taxes accounted for only 29 percent of the total taxes in Beverly and 25 percent in Wenham.[11] As the taxation of persons declined, property became more heavily taxed. In Beverly, personal property, which included ships, farm implements, and money at interest, increased in its assessment value from 1771 to 1790. Indeed, in 1771 a new category appeared on the tax lists: "money at interest." Only a few years earlier, all commercial property appeared as personal property. By 1790, personal property and money at interest amounted to almost one-third of the total taxes in Beverly; in 1741, it was only 11 percent. Yet in Wenham, real property taxes increasingly accounted for total taxation. By 1790, they were 70 percent of the total taxes, while in 1741, real and personal property each amounted to 26 percent of the total. During this period, the farm lands, meadows, houses, and woodlands of Wenham became more valuable. As Wenham's economy remained agricultural, taxation of land meant that owning and controlling farms would become more expensive. But in nearby Beverly, the tax base of the town was more diversified, combining commercial and agricultural growth.

As a result of these changes, Beverly, much more than

FIGURE 1–1. Real and Personal Property Taxes as Percentages of Total Taxes: Beverly and Wenham Compared, 1731–1790

Wenham, became stratified. While the distribution of wealth was unequal in both towns, as those at the top of the economic ladder controlled more property, wealth inequality increased more substantially in Beverly than in Wenham, particularly after the Revolution. Between 1741 and 1771, the distribution of real property in both towns was remarkably similar (see Table 1–3).[12] The wealthiest 20 percent of the male taxpayers controlled between 50 and 60 percent of the real property in each town. Those in the bottom fortieth percentile owned only 4 percent of the real property. Overall, however, about one-fourth of the male taxpayers of each town owned no land at all, although they were taxed as laborers. Compared with Wenham, Beverly's distribution of real property was slightly more stratified, as more people ranked at the top and fewer ranked in the middle. By 1790, this differential increased as the

TABLE 1–3. *The Distribution of Real and Personal Property in Beverly and Wenham during the Eighteenth Century*

Percentage of the Population	Percentage of Real Property[a]					
	1741		1771		1790	
	Beverly[b]	Wenham[c]	Beverly[b]	Wenham[c]	Beverly[b]	Wenham[c]
Top 20%	61%	52%	61%	55%	70%	57%
Mid 40%	36%	45%	34%	40%	28%	42%
Low 40%	4%	4%	4%	5%	2%	2%
Top 10%	39%	39%	41%	34%	49%	36%
	Percentage of Personal Property					
Top 20%	65%	57%	92%	51%	89%	59%
Mid 40%	34%	39%	6%	45%	11%	41%
Low 40%	2%	4%	3%	5%	1%	0
Top 10%	45%	38%	87%	31%	79%	37%
N	(307)	(113)	(462)	(98)	(619)	(94)

[a] Tax lists provided the sources for real property distributions in each town. Provincial tax lists were used for each town, and the total N included here represents resident, male, taxpayers.

[b] The 1741 and 1771 lists for Beverly were taken from Beverly Tax Data, Tax and Valuation Lists of Massachusetts Towns Before 1776, Microfilm copy, reel 10, Lamont Library, Harvard University, Cambridge, Mass. The 1790 tax lists are from Tax Lists of Beverly, 1790–97, Assessors' Office, City Hall, Beverly, Mass.

[c] The 1741 and 1771 lists for Wenham were taken from Wenham Tax Data, Tax and Valuation Lists of Massachusetts Towns Before 1776, Microfilm copy, reel 11, Lamont Library, Harvard University, Cambridge, Mass. The 1790 tax lists are from Town Records of Wenham, Taxes, vol. II, 1783–1803, Town Clerk's Office, Town Hall, Wenham, Mass.

wealthiest 20 percent of Beverly's taxpayers controlled 70 percent of the real property. This increase came primarily at the expense of the men in the middle, whose proportions declined. In Wenham, though, the distribution of real property remained the same in 1790 as it had been before the Revolution.

The stratification of Beverly's economy became even more evident in the distribution of personal property. In 1741, the distribution of personal property was only slightly more stratified in Beverly than in Wenham. By 1771, the top 20 percent of the taxpayers of Beverly controlled 92 percent of the personal property of the town, a pattern of inequality that held true nineteen years later. In contrast, Wenham's distribution of personal property remained stable.

The sources of the unequal distributions of wealth in Beverly and Wenham were twofold: first, merchants and traders accumulated more commercial property; and, second, the propertyless tended to be younger sons waiting to inherit family property. In both Beverly and Wenham, the proportions of taxpayers who owned no property remained substantially the same between 1741 and 1761, averaging about one-fourth of the male taxpayers.[13] Only in 1771 was there a slight increase in the proportions of men who did not own personal property, up from 20 to 27 percent in Beverly, and from 13 to 24 percent in Wenham. Landlessness—that is, nonownership of real property—had become more consistent in both towns. This evidence suggests that the shift in stratification in Beverly, and to a much lesser degree in Wenham, was the result of an expanded merchant and trader class, not the creation of a new group of propertyless men at the bottom.

Younger men in both towns had to wait their turns to gain access to wealth. In Beverly, there was an inverse relationship between the wealth rank of fathers and sons, with many more young men ranking at the bottom of the economic ladder while their fathers were at the top. This same inverse relationship occurred in Wenham, where not even one father ranked in the bottom fortieth percentile. Landlessness, to some extent, was a matter of age and the stage of one's life; young men gradually came of age and gained access to economic resources. But sons had more opportunities in Beverly than in Wenham, because of its commercial economy.[14]

The occupational structures of the two towns reflected this difference. In the three northeastern seaports of Boston, New

York, and Philadelphia,[15] the service sector was much more developed than the industrial or maritime sectors. In smaller seaports like Beverly, the service sector of the economy was less developed than the maritime sector; seamen and fishermen dominated the occupational structure of eighteenth-century Beverly, while services were more dispersed among the other seaports of the county. In Essex County, the smaller ports like Beverly did not exactly replicate the occupational structures of the large ports like Boston. Rather, they developed particular sectors of the commercial economy; in the case of Beverly, the maritime and shipping sector. Eighteenth-century Wenham, in contrast, maintained an agricultural economy and continued to rely on neighboring seaport towns for its market needs.

The evidence on the occupational structures of Beverly and Wenham derives from records of the Essex County Probate Court and the lists of men and women who died in each town. To be sure, this evidence is an imperfect record of all the occupations to be found in the two towns. Yet by examining this evidence over a long span of time, from 1681 to 1840, one can see the changes and continuities in occupations in the village and seaport.[16] (See Plate 1–2.)

Over the course of the eighteenth century, the proportions of men in Beverly who worked in maritime and shipping occupations remained fairly steady at about 25 percent (see Table 1–4). During the early nineteenth century, however, the maritime sector of the economy increased substantially to 35 percent. Simultaneously, the agricultural sector of Beverly's economy declined, from 34 percent in 1721–1760 to 16 percent in 1801–1840. The proportions of tradesmen, gentlemen, and women who died holding property all increased over the eighteenth century. Beverly became a truly mixed commercial and agricultural town, as farmers, fishermen, and tradesmen all plied their trades together. The steadily increasing numbers of men and women who died in the town, as shown in Figure 1–2,

TABLE 1–4. *Occupational Structure of Beverly, 1680–1840: Evidence from the Probate Records*

Occupation	1681–1720	1721–1760	1761–1800	1801–1840
Gentlemen	—	2%	8%	6%
Professionals	6%	1%	2%	1%
Trade	—	1%	3%	6%
Maritime	29%	21%	27%	35%
Artisans	18%	22%	16%	14%
Agricultural	33%	34%	24%	16%
Laborers	—	—	—	1%
Women	15%	19%	21%	21%
N	(55)	(140)	(337)	(632)

SOURCE: Essex County Probate Docket, 1638–1840, Essex County Court House, Salem, Mass.

supports the fact that Beverly's economy was growing during the middle and end of the eighteenth century.

In contrast, the almost level line of deaths in Wenham reiterates the relative stagnation of the economy there. Its population failed to grow, and its economy remained unchanged. Over one-half of the men who died in mid-eighteenth-century Wenham were either husbandmen or yeomen. After 1761, the proportions of husbandmen and yeomen declined, while the proportions of gentlemen rose sharply (see Table 1–5). If we consider gentlemen as farmers, then the proportion of farmers in Wenham in 1721–1760 was 63 percent, and 69 percent in 1801–1840. A few artisans lived in the town, particularly those who fit into the daily needs of village life: bricklayers, coopers, joiners, masons, and housewrights. Beverly had thirty-one different kinds of artisans; Wenham, nine. There were only three innholders in Wenham and one merchant. In such a small, agricultural town like Wenham, wealth differences manifested themselves less in terms of commercial versus farming interests than in terms of social status, as the proportions of men who

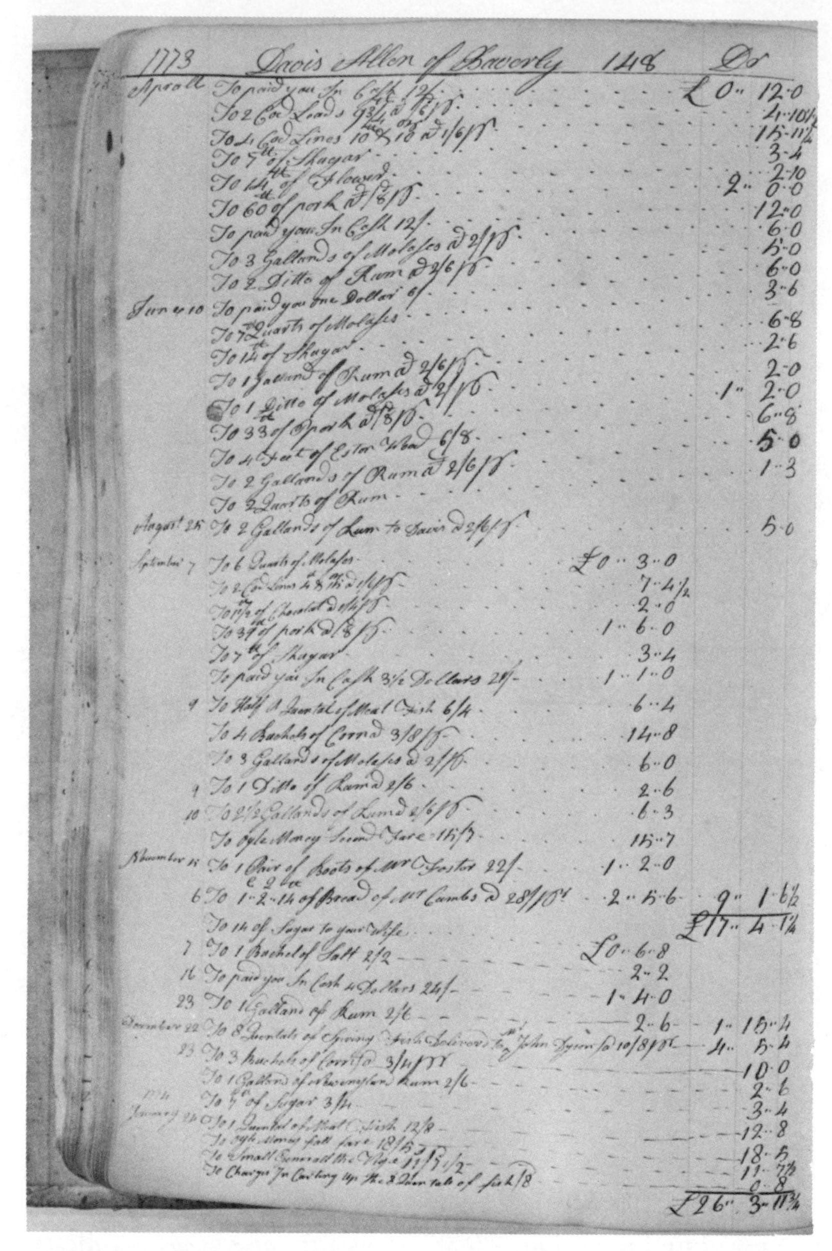

1773 Davis Allen of Beverly 148 Dr

Date	Item	£ s d	£ s d
Aprill	To paid you for 6 [illegible] 12/		£0.. 12·0
	To 2 Cod Leads 9¾ at 6/		4·10½
	To 4 Cod Lines 10 & 10 at 1/6		15·11½
	To 7 lb of Shagar		3·4
	To 14 lb of Flower		2·10
	To 60 lb of pork at /8		2.. 0·0
	To paid you In Cash 12/		12·0
	To 3 Gallands of Molasses at 2/		6·0
	To 2 Ditto of Rum at 2/6		5·0
June 10	To paid you one Dollar 6/		6·0
	To 7 Quarts of Molasses		3·6
	To 14 lb of Shagar		6·8
	To 1 Gallond of Rum at 2/6		2·6
	To 1 Ditto of Molasses at 2/		2·0
	To 33 lb of pork at /8		1.. 2·0
	To 4 Feet of Ester Board 6/8		6··8
	To 2 Gallands of Rum at 2/6		5·0
	To 2 Quarts of Rum		1··3
August 25	To 2 Gallands of Rum to Davis at 2/6		5·0
September 7	To 6 Quarts of Molasses	£0 .. 3 .. 0	
	To 2 Cod Lines	7 .. 4½	
	To 1½ of Chocolat	2 .. 0	
	To 39 of pork at /8	1 .. 6 .. 0	
	To 7 lb of Shagar	3 .. 4	
	To paid you In Cash 3½ Dollars 21/	1 .. 1 .. 0	
9	To Half A Quintal of Meal Fish 6/4	6 .. 4	
	To 4 Bushels of Corn at 3/8	14 .. 8	
	To 3 Gallands of Molasses at 2/	6 .. 0	
9	To 1 Ditto of Rum at 2/6	2 .. 6	
10	To 2½ Gallands of Rum at 2/6	6 .. 3	
	To [illegible] Money Second Fare 15/7	15 .. 7	
November 15	To 1 Pair of Boots of Mr Foster 22/	1 .. 2 .. 0	
6	To 1-2-14 of Bread of Mr Combs at 28/10	2 .. 5 .. 6	9 .. 1·6½
			£17 .. 4·1¼
	To 14 of Sugar to your Wife	£0 .. 6 .. 8	
7	To 1 Bushel of Salt 2/2	2 .. 2	
16	To paid you In Cash 4 Dollars 24/	1 .. 4 .. 0	
23	To 1 Gallond of Rum 2/6	2 .. 6	1 .. 15 .. 4
December 22	To 8 Quintals of Spring Fish Delivered to Mr John [illegible] at 10/8		4 .. 5·4
23	To 3 Bushels of Corn at 3/4		10·0
	To 1 Gallond of Newengland Rum 2/6		2·6
1774	To 7 lb of Sugar 3/4		3·4
January 24	To 1 Quintal of Meal Fish 12/8		12·8
	To 5th Money Salt Fare 18/5		18·5
	To Small General the Voyage 11/7½		11·7½
	To Charges for Carting up the 8 Quintals of Fish /8		0·8
			£26 .. 3 .. 11¾

PLATE 1–2. Pages from the account book of Captain Thomas Davis of Beverly. The left-hand page lists the supplies that Davis provided to Davis Allen for a voyage and personal use,

while the right-hand side shows that Allen promised part of his catch (or "fare") in payment. Courtesy Essex Institute, Salem, Massachusetts.

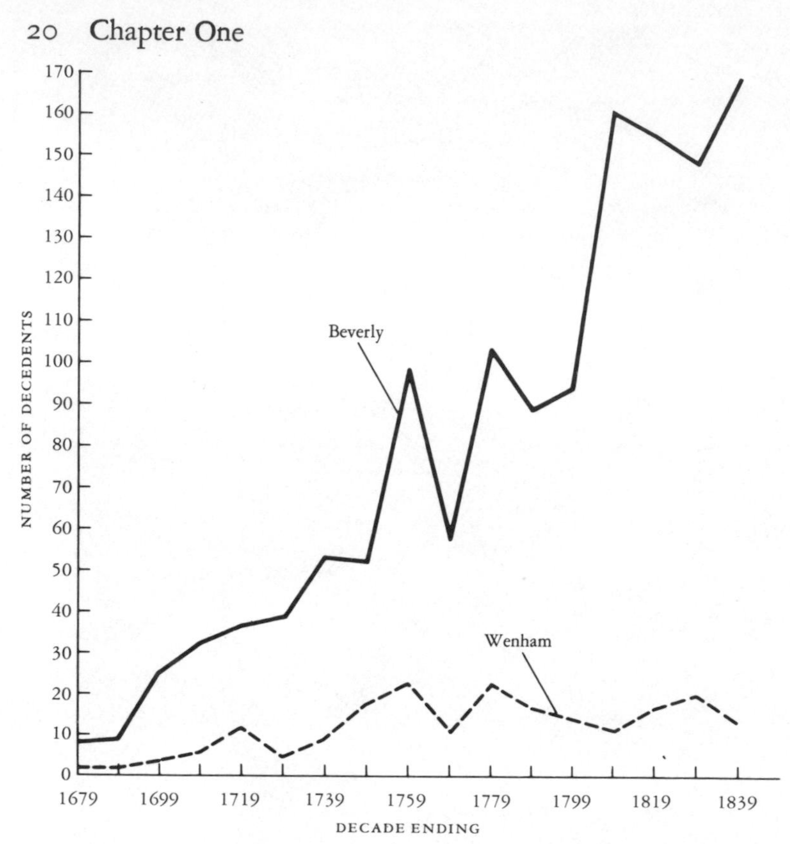

FIGURE 1–2. Probated Deaths in Beverly and Wenham, 1679–1839

used the title of "gentlemen" bear out. Wenham may have had a stable distribution of wealth over the eighteenth century, but gentlemen doubled in their proportion of the whole by the early nineteenth century.

Within the regional economy of eighteenth-century Essex County, Beverly symbolized commercial growth and Wenham the limits of agricultural development. The commercialization of seaport towns like Beverly went hand in hand with an increasingly stratified distribution of wealth.[17] Whereas once the two towns had been roughly similar, now one grew while the other stagnated. The farmers of Wenham were set in their path

TABLE 1–5. *Occupational Structure of Wenham, 1680–1840: Evidence from the Probate Records*

Occupation	1681–1720	1721–1760	1761–1800	1801–1840
Gentlemen	—	14%	21%	31%
Professionals	9%	5%	3%	3%
Trade	—	5%	2%	2%
Maritime	9%	3%	8%	2%
Artisans	27%	3%	18%	5%
Agricultural	46%	49%	31%	38%
Women	9%	22%	16%	20%
N	(11)	(37)	(61)	(61)

SOURCE: Essex County Probate Docket, 1638–1840, Essex County Court House, Salem, Mass.

toward agricultural stability, while Beverly's merchants, traders, fishermen, and farmers participated in building a more commercially oriented economy. In doing so, the people of Beverly provided the means for adapting to the pressures of population growth and migration within the economic structure of the town. In contrast, the people of Wenham began to search for additional agricultural resources, which ultimately meant limiting the opportunities within the town or moving elsewhere. In these two eighteenth-century towns, the effects of population growth and migration came to be viewed differently, for the people of Beverly brought a more complex economic structure to bear on the pressures of a growing population, while the farmers of Wenham coped as best they could with diminishing resources.

CHAPTER 2

SOURCES OF POPULATION GROWTH

IN 1790, William Bentley, the Salem diarist, observed one of the primary changes occurring in eighteenth-century Massachusetts: increased migration. Touching both the rich and the poor, increased mobility had become a way of life in eighteenth-century Salem, resulting in a realignment of the rules for defining the social order. Bentley noted that the Salem selectmen debated "whether or not to warn Strangers out of Town in order to save the Town from the Charges of the Poor." But the poor were not the only migrants in Salem. Bentley also observed that it "is found in fact that the greater part of the whole property is in the hands of persons not Town born, and in the best streets even a majority of freeholders are newcomers."[1] Bentley's observations were less the particularistic sentiments of a local diarist than the perceptions of an astute commentator reflecting on the effects of differential economic growth in Massachusetts.

POPULATION GROWTH IN MASSACHUSETTS

The primary demographic characteristic of the white population of colonial Massachusetts was rapid growth. In a classically Malthusian configuration of low ages at marriage, generally uncontrolled fertility practices, and a healthy environment, the white population expanded at fluctuating but consistently high levels in almost every decade, particularly during the eighteenth century (see Table 2–1).[2] By 1770, though, the decennial growth rates in Massachusetts began to decline sharply. These decreased levels of growth after 1770 were not merely artifacts of the disruptions of the Revolutionary War; modest

TABLE 2–1. *Decennial Growth Rates of the White Population of Massachusetts, 1660–1860*

Decade	Total Population	Percent Decennial Change
1660[a]	20,082	—
1670	30,000	49.6%
1680	39,752	32.5%
1690	49,504	24.5%
1700	55,941	13.0%
1710	62,390	11.5%
1720	91,008	45.9%
1730	114,116	25.4%
1740	151,613	32.9%
1750	188,000	23.9%
1760	222,600	23.5%
1770	235,308	5.7%
1780	268,627	14.2%
1790[b]	373,324	—[c]
1800	416,393	11.5%
1810	465,203	11.7%
1820	516,419	11.1%
1830	603,359	16.8%
1840	729,030	20.8%
1850	985,450	35.2%
1860	1,221,432	23.5%

[a] Data for 1660–1780 are taken from U.S. Bureau of the Census, *Historical Statistics of the United States, Colonial Times to 1957* (Washington, D.C.: Government Printing Office, 1960), 756, Series Z 1–19.

[b] Population totals for the period 1790–1860 are taken from U.S. Bureau of the Census, *First Census,* 33; *Second Census,* 12; *Third Census,* 12a; *Fourth Census,* Book I, 5; *Fifth Census,* 20–21; *Sixth Census,* 8–9; *Seventh Census,* 48; *Eighth Census,* 226, Table 4. The population in 1860 includes all races.

[c] Because the data from 1790–1860 are not estimated, the percentage change from 1780–1790 was omitted.

rates of population growth prevailed throughout the early decades of the nineteenth century as well. Not until after 1840, when European immigrants swelled the size of the Massachusetts population, did rates of growth similar to those of the eighteenth century reappear. The worst fear of Malthus—famine as a result of overpopulation—never occurred in colonial New England. Rather, one of the more prominent effects of population growth in Massachusetts was internal migration.

Historians of migration are most familiar with foreign immigration as the major component of population growth in America. This fact is best seen in the expanding nineteenth-century city, which teemed with new faces from abroad and from rural America. Yet in colonial Massachusetts population growth occurred primarily from within as families expanded to their biologically maximum sizes. But with increasing population growth also came pressures upon available economic resources. If population growth was the central demographic fact of eighteenth-century Massachusetts, then internal migration was its major corollary. For the people of eighteenth-century Massachusetts, migration became an adaptive process that facilitated the redistribution of economic resources, creating a new equilibrium between resources and people. In 1765, for example, four-fifths of the population of Massachusetts lived in the eastern counties. Thirty-five years later, migration redistributed the population so that the eastern counties contained only 60 percent of the population. Migration within Massachusetts as well as movement to newly settled lands such as New Hampshire and Maine reduced the overall growth rate of the population. During the late eighteenth century, rates of population growth in Maine and New Hampshire greatly exceeded those of Massachusetts. Without efficient fertility control, migration in eighteenth-century Massachusetts became for many a stop-gap attempt to limit the size of the population and to redistribute economic resources.[3]

It is unlikely that the steady growth of the New England population was the result of increased levels of foreign immigration.[4] Despite some qualitative evidence which seems to support this view, the sustained growth of the Massachusetts population, and its subsequent decline in 1770, cannot be attributed to fluctuations in foreign immigration. Although large numbers of immigrants entered the American colonies during the eighteenth century, few entered New England.[5] Evidence from the surviving indentures to American colonies from eighteenth-century London records indicates that less than 1 percent of the laborers (most of whom were males) entered New England. The middle and southern colonies and the Caribbean Islands accounted for over 95 percent of the bound labor from London. Even as early as the 1680s, London records revealed only 1 percent of the servants immigrating to New England.[6] Rather than growth from foreign immigration, the population of Massachusetts expanded from within. Moreover, the very fact that few bound servants from London actually landed in New England suggests that there was an extremely small demand for labor, reinforcing the conclusion that population and resources became imbalanced. From an English perspective, New England was not the land of opportunity in the eighteenth century.

While the overall rate of population growth in Massachusetts was high, there still was variation in those rates in Beverly and Wenham. Some towns expanded rapidly, others remained stable, and some actually lost people as the combined effects of population growth and availability of economic resources led people to migrate.

THE COMPONENTS OF POPULATION GROWTH

Population growth in late eighteenth-century Essex County generally reflected the high levels of growth found in Massachusetts as a whole. The population in Essex County decreased at the end of the eighteenth century, remained at low levels during the first three decades of the nineteenth century, and expanded again after 1840. Yet within Essex County, Beverly and Wenham grew at strikingly different rates (see Table 2–2).

Wenham's pattern of growth represented the extremes of depopulation. In 1741, its growth rate was only 15 percent, well below the Massachusetts total of 33 percent. A mere decade later, the population of Wenham actually declined by

TABLE 2–2. *Decennial Growth Rates of the White Populations of Beverly, Wenham, and Essex County, Massachusetts, before 1860*

	Beverly		Wenham		Essex County	
Year	Total Population	Percent Change	Total Population	Percent Change	Total Population	Percent Change
1731[a]	n.a.	—	553	—	n.a.	—
1741	1517	—	639	+16%	n.a.	—
1751	1418	– 7%	522	–18%	n.a.	—
1761[b]	1859	+31%	549	+ 5%	n.a.	—
1771	2462	+32%	544	– 1%	n.a.	—
1790[c]	3232	—	492	—	57,033	—
1800	3789	+17%	468	– 5%	60,285	+ 6%
1810	4547	+17%	549	+17%	71,028	+18%
1820	4269	– 6%	568	+ 2%	75,483	+ 6%
1830	4051	– 5%	610	+ 7%	82,336	+ 9%
1840	4666	+15%	689	+13%	94,480	+15%
1850	5360	+15%	973	+41%	130,677	+38%
1860[d]	6147	+15%	1101	+13%	165,611	+27%

[a] Population figures for Beverly and Wenham during the period 1731–1771 were estimated by multiplying the number of male polls listed in tax lists by 4.5.

[b] In 1753, the boundaries of Beverly were enlarged by the annexation of part of Salem.

[c] Population figures for Beverly, Wenham, and Essex County from 1790–1860 are taken from U.S. Bureau of the Census, *First Census*, 33; *Second Census*, 12; *Third Census*, 12a; *Fourth Census*, Book I, 5; *Fifth Census*, 20–21; *Sixth Census*, 8–9; *Seventh Census*, 48; *Eighth Census*, 226, Table 4.

[d] The population of Essex County in 1860 includes all races.

over 18 percent. This rapid depopulation continued throughout the eighteenth century and into the early nineteenth century. A small spurt of growth occurred between 1800 and 1810, but this recovery was shortlived. Rather, there was a long-term decline in the population of Wenham from the middle of the eighteenth century until 1840, almost 100 years of minimal levels of population growth in an era of high fertility. Obviously, out-migration took its toll on the size of the Wenham population.

Beverly's pattern of population growth between 1750 and 1840 was more complex than Wenham's. Up to 1751, when evidence is first available in a consistent time series, it appears as though Beverly also suffered the effects of depopulation. Between 1741 and 1751, Beverly's population declined by 7 percent. But in 1753, Beverly expanded its town boundaries by gaining a part of Salem called Royalside. The Salem petitioners had exercised what had become a familiar request in colonial New England: the desire to live closer to the meeting house of Beverly than the one in Salem.[7] One suspects, though, that beneath the petitioners' request was an economic concern. Most of the signers were tied to the commercial networks of Beverly: gentlemen, a merchant, an innholder, a blacksmith, a cordwainer, and several yeomen. In the years following Beverly's expansion, the town's population grew rapidly, over 30 percent per decade. But in the early nineteenth century, the town's population did not rise as sharply as it had in the twenty years before the Revolution. Still, compared with Wenham, the population of Beverly was dynamic. As a small seaport, Beverly's population tended to rise and fall with the general economic swings associated with commerce more directly than Wenham's. Beverly's population fell off sharply, for example, during and after the War of 1812, while Wenham's made some modest gains.

Two points should be underscored here: first, both Beverly

and Wenham lost population during the 1740s; and, second, Wenham's population declined more dramatically and consistently than Beverly's. Despite the location of each town in eastern Massachusetts, Wenham's farmers experienced the extremes of depopulation while Beverly's farmers, artisans, and mariners expanded their numbers.

What were the sources of population growth and change in Beverly and Wenham? One way to analyze population movement between two time periods is the residual or net method.[8] This technique, although appropriate to the evidence from Beverly and Wenham, also has its limitations. It nevertheless is useful to portray the contributions to net population change of natural growth and migration—the two processes that cause growth or decline in a population. For purposes of comparison, the net population changes among the male taxpayers in Beverly and Wenham between 1761 and 1771 will be considered. The conclusions are startling: patterns of net population growth in Beverly and Wenham present two contrasting views of change in these two eighteenth-century eastern Massachusetts towns. Wenham, the small, landlocked, farming town, was gripped by a demographic crisis. Despite comparable fertility patterns in each town, maturing sons comprised only a small part of the total increase of men in Wenham.[9] In Beverly, however, maturing sons contributed substantially to the town's population growth during the 1760s.

Unlike the late nineteenth-century American pattern of urban net population growth, which depended heavily on migration, eighteenth-century Beverly grew from an excess of births against deaths. The total number of male taxpayers in Beverly increased by 23 percent between 1761 and 1771 (see Table 2–3). Net migration, on the other hand, was negative in Beverly. In-migration contributed nothing to the growth of Beverly, at least according to the net method of analysis, while maturing sons caused the population to bulge in only one decade.

TABLE 2–3. *Net Components of Population Growth in Beverly and in Wenham, 1761–1771*

Beverly, 1761–1771		Wenham, 1761–1771	
1761 male taxpayers	368	1761 male taxpayers	99
1771 male taxpayers	454	1771 male taxpayers	98
Total change	+86	Total change	−1
Percentage change	+23%	Percentage change	−1%
Natural increase	+94	Natural increase	+7
Net migration	− 8	Net migration	−8
Natural increase as percentage of 1761	+26%	Natural increase as percentage of 1761	+7%
Net migration as percentage of 1761	− 2%	Net migration as percentage of 1761	−8%

SOURCES: Beverly and Wenham tax lists and reconstitution data.

In contrast, Wenham's net population growth between 1761 and 1771 reflected heavy out-migration and minimal movement by newcomers. Wenham's overall population size was static, declining only 1 percent, as maturing sons failed to increase the size of the population. The natural increase of matured sons in Wenham was only 7 percent, as compared with 26 percent in Beverly. Net migration changes in Wenham were important, however, in that out-migration accounted for the stable population size. The only similarity between Beverly and Wenham suggested by the net method of analysis was the relatively minor role of net migration as a component of overall growth. Superficially, both Beverly and Wenham appear to have been insular towns, relatively unaffected by the flow of in-migrants.

This picture of insularity in Beverly and Wenham based on negative levels of net migration is deceptively simple. It is one thing to say that net migration contributed little to the decennial growth rates in Beverly and Wenham. It is quite another to infer insularity from minimal net migration. Although net migration rates in Beverly and Wenham indicate the contribution of migration to total net growth, they reveal little about the actual flows of migrants.[10] In other words, the net method of analysis focuses primarily on the sources of overall population growth but does not portray the extent of migration occurring within the decade, the size of the migratory flows, nor the characteristics of newcomers and maturing sons. In order to know if eighteenth-century Beverly and Wenham were truly insular, we must examine the streams of persons who entered and exited these towns.

Of the new men who entered the tax lists, matured sons comprised 22 to 32 percent of the taxpayers in both towns (see Table 2–4). Native sons were least likely to find a place in Wenham during the decade of 1741–1751, and overall, more maturing sons continued to live in Beverly than did those in Wenham. In 1751, for example, maturing sons in Beverly comprised 32 percent of the taxpayers, while in Wenham, they represented only 22 percent. The pressures of population growth fell more heavily on the sons of Wenham's farmers, so that fewer of them could gain land and the status of a taxpayer. The few native sons who did gain access to wealth were younger than their counterparts in Beverly. In Wenham, matured sons had a mean age of twenty-five years in 1761 and twenty-four in 1771. In Beverly the mean ages of matured sons were twenty-seven and twenty-six years, respectively. With population pressures more severe in Wenham, it appears as though fathers passed their wealth—usually land—on to sons at an early age, at least compared with Beverly. But in Beverly, with proportionally more maturing sons achieving the status of taxpayers, one could presume that there were greater economic opportunities available.

Compared with in-migrants, matured sons predominated among the new taxpayers in both Beverly and Wenham. Still, in-migration was a constant fact of life in Beverly, with newcomers averaging about 20 percent of all taxpayers between

TABLE 2–4. *Components of Population Turnover in Beverly and in Wenham, 1731–1771*

Components of Population Turnover	Year of Taxpayer's Appearance					
	1731	1741	1751	1761	1771	Total
Decade of first appearance						
Matured sons						
Beverly	—	—	32%	29%	30%	30%
Wenham	—	28%	22%	24%	24%	24%
In-migrants[a]						
Beverly	—	—	18%	23%	18%	20%
Wenham	—	12%	15%	19%	16%	16%
Decade of last appearance						
Deaths						
Beverly	—	24%	22%	11%	—	19%
Wenham	11%	12%	24%	16%	—	16%
Out-migrants[a]						
Beverly	—	27%	21%	25%	—	24%
Wenham	21%	29%	23%	24%	—	25%
Persisters[b]						
Beverly	—	50%	58%	64%	—	57%
Wenham	68%	58%	53%	60%	—	60%
Total male taxpayers						
Beverly	—	(302)	(304)	(368)	(454)	(1428)
Wenham	(99)	(113)	(105)	(99)	(98)	(514)

SOURCES: Beverly and Wenham tax lists and reconstitution data.

[a] As used in this table, in- and out-migrants include the maximum estimate, which involved assuming that unknowns were counted as migrants. For a full discussion of this procedure, see the Appendix. In summary, an analysis of the length of residence, mortality, and wealth characteristics of known and unknown taxpayers revealed that the latter were more likely to be migrants rather than persons who had died. Any other alternative would have biased the analysis in favor of residential continuity.

[b] The persistence statistic displayed in this table represents the proportion of the taxpayer population which was living in each town ten years after the date of appearance.

1741 and 1771. Migration increased in Wenham as the eighteenth century progressed. From an initially small flow of in-migrants in 1741 of only 12 percent, newcomers increased to 19 percent by 1761. The larger flow of newcomers was possibly related to the French and Indian War, for Beverly also had more new taxpayers that year. From the perspective of the components of population turnover, though, in-migrants were a real presence in each of the towns. Unlike the net method of analysis of population change, which stressed the minimal importance of newcomers, a closer look at those entering the towns reveals that newcomers were a normal part of the daily life of Beverly and were increasingly important in Wenham.

Although this evidence does not reveal the total volume of population turnover, it appears as though nearly one-fifth of the taxpayers were newcomers. Insularity, as suggested by the net analysis of population change, was not the dominant theme in the turnover of the people of Beverly and Wenham. For a town as small as Wenham, with about 100 male taxpayers, the addition of 15 and 20 new persons could materially affect the life of the town. In Beverly, though, with its larger population, newcomers were probably less visible.

As a group, newcomers were older than maturing sons in both towns, averaging about thirty-five years of age in 1761 and twenty-nine years a decade later. These eighteenth-century newcomers to Beverly and Wenham were older than one might expect, particularly given the relatively youthful ages of migrants in modern America.[11] Many of these in-migrants were wealthier than others, perhaps accounting for their older ages as a group.

Movement into Beverly and Wenham during the mid-eighteenth century was surpassed only by out-migration. While nearly one-fifth of the male taxpayers who arrived every decade were newcomers, about one-fourth of the taxpayers left town. The proportions of taxpayers moving out of Beverly and Wenham were more similar than different. Each town had slightly higher-than-average rates of out-migration during the decade 1741–1751, and slightly lower rates ten years later, during the French and Indian War. Overall, mobility from these two towns was more common than movement into them. In particular, Wenham lost twice as many taxpayers between 1731 and 1751 as compared with newcomers who entered during the same period. Beverly's flow of out-migrants also outnumbered its newcomers, but less dramatically than Wenham's.

Out-migrants from Beverly were slightly younger than those from Wenham, although as a group these eighteenth-century out-migrants seem older than one might expect. In Beverly, they averaged about thirty-three years of age in 1761; in Wenham their average age was thirty-seven years. The higher average ages of out-migrants is best explained by the fact that our taxpayers, as a group, were an adult population. Many younger sons simply migrated out-of-town without ever appearing on a tax list. On the other hand, the evidence presented here suggests that both newcomers and out-migrants were willing to migrate at older ages. Out-migration was clearly an important component of the demographic structure of eighteenth-century Beverly and Wenham.

MIGRATION AND MORTALITY

With Wenham experiencing depopulation during the eighteenth century, and Beverly's population increasing, the relationship of mortality to patterns of growth and decline becomes an important question. In both towns, the overall proportions of out-migrants exceeded those who died during the mid-eighteenth century (see Table 2–4). Particularly in Wenham, adult taxpayers tended to leave town rather than spend their lives there. The ratio of out-migrants to persons who died was almost two to one in Wenham, with the exception of the decade of the French and Indian War, 1751 to 1761. More generally, out-migration depleted the population of Wenham, not mortality. In sharp

TABLE 2–5. *Mean Ages at Death of Adults in Beverly, by Selected Characteristics, 1661–1760*

Characteristics	Birth Cohorts 1661–1720	Birth Cohorts 1721–1760	Effect and F-test Significance	Proportion of Variance
Adult males	63.7 (170)	59.2 (175)	—	—
Persisters and migrants				
Matured sons	63.8 (61)	58.2 (148)		
In-migrants	71.7 (24)	62.1 (26)	NS	—
Nonmigrants	64.0 (139)	42.2 (23)		
Out-migrants	74.0 (23)	65.4 (25)	NS	—
Real property rank				
Top 40%	68.6 (119)	62.5 (58)	Real under 0.001	3.2%
Low 60%	60.8 (50)	56.9 (117)	Cohort under 0.05	1.7%
Personal property rank				
Top 40%	69.1 (102)	61.9 (61)	Personal under 0.01	2.8%
Low 60%	61.9 (67)	57.2 (114)	Cohort under 0.01	2.7%

TABLE 2–5. (*continued*).

Characteristics	Birth Cohorts 1661–1720		Birth Cohorts 1721–1760		Effect and F-test Significance	Proportion of Variance
Adult females						
Real property of husband						
Top 40%	60.5	(43)	60.8	(23)	NS	—
Low 60%	53.3	(18)	60.9	(49)		
Personal property of husband						
Top 40%	58.1	(39)	59.0	(26)	NS	—
Low 60%	58.9	(22)	61.9	(46)		

SOURCE: Beverly tax lists and reconstitution data.

NOTE: The two-way analysis of variance used in this table is a factorial design based on two independent variables and one dependent variable, mean age at death. Each of the independent variables in the left-hand column, "Characteristics," was analyzed in relation to the independent variable birth cohort. The mean ages at death for adult men and women are reported for each of the two groups of persons within each birth cohort, 1661–1720 and 1721–1760. The next column presents the "effect" of each variable on mean age at death, or, the "interaction effect" of the two independent variables on age at death. Also reported in this column is the significance level of the F-test (if at the 0.05 level). If not, the designation "NS" (not significant) is used to show lack of statistical significance. This designation is also used to denote relationships where the total number of cases was too small to warrant their inclusion, although the mean age at death is reported. The last column gives the proportion of the variance in mean age at death accounted for by the variable with the main effect of or the interaction of the two independent variables.

Wealth rankings in this table are those of last appearance of male taxpayers.

contrast to Wenham, the population of Beverly changed both by migration and mortality. Between 1741 and 1761, the proportions of deaths and out-migrants almost balanced each other. Only between 1761 and 1771 did the proportion of taxpayers who died decline while migration remained at its usual level.

The seaport was a less healthy environment than the village.[12] By using the mean age at death as an indicator of length of life, we may approximate the impact of wealth and occupational status on mortality.[13] Overall, the mean age at death of male taxpayers in Beverly declined between the seventeenth and eighteenth centuries, from sixty-four years for those born before 1720, to fifty-nine years for those born between 1721 and 1760 (see Table 2–5). This same pattern of decline occurred in Wenham, as the mean age at death dropped from sixty-nine to sixty-two years (see Table 2–6). By the mid-eighteenth century, mean ages at death in village and seaport were more similar than they had been before 1720. This downward trend in the mean age at death was true for maturing sons, in-migrants, and out-migrants in both towns.[14]

While mean ages at death were not that different among migrants and maturing sons, there were more apparent variations according to wealth rank. In Beverly, men ranking at the bottom of the economic ladder died at younger average ages than those at the top. These wealth differences in age at death among taxpayers held true both for those born before 1720 and those born later. One's economic status *and* the general decline in the age at death combined to lower the average age at death of male taxpayers in Beverly. In contrast to Beverly, male taxpayers in Wenham died at lower ages after 1720 as a result of the general decline in mortality and not because of economic differences. Although there was a five to six year difference in the mean age at death among men at the top and bottom of the tax lists, that differential resulted from an overall decline in the age of death rather than absolute wealth differences.

TABLE 2–6. *Mean Ages at Death of Adults in Wenham, by Selected Characteristics, 1661–1760*

Characteristics	Birth Cohorts 1661–1720		Birth Cohorts 1721–1760		Effect and F-test Significance	Proportion of Variance
Adult males	69.4	(82)	61.9	(40)	—	—
Persisters and migrants						
Matured sons	69.5	(46)	62.2	(34)	NS	—
In-migrants	69.4	(11)	60.5	(6)		
Nonmigrants	72.8	(58)	56.6	(23)		
Out-migrants	65.9	(22)	70.9	(11)	NS	—
Real property rank						
Top 40%	70.0	(42)	65.9	(15)	Cohort under 0.01	6.4%
Low 60%	72.2	(40)	59.6	(25)		
Personal property rank						
Top 40%	69.9	(42)	64.8	(17)	Cohort under 0.01	7.2%
Low 60%	72.2	(40)	59.8	(23)		
Adult females						
Real property of husband						
Top 40%	59.5	(13)	84.0	(4)		
Low 60%	47.6	(12)	56.6	(14)	NS	—
Personal property of husband						
Top 40%	57.8	(12)	80.0	(6)		
Low 60%	50.0	(13)	54.0	(12)	NS	—

SOURCE: Wenham tax lists and reconstitution data.
NOTE: See note to Table 2–5 for explanation of this table.

With their seafaring occupations, many of the taxpayers of Beverly were exposed to the hazards of maritime life. The mean age at death among mariners in Beverly during the last half of the eighteenth century was only fifty-one years. Artisans died at an average age of fifty-five years, while gentlemen, professionals, tradesmen, and farmers died on the average at sixty-six years of age.[15] The importance of maritime deaths in the turnover of Beverly's population can be seen from a contemporary source: over one-third of the adult, male deaths in Beverly between 1741 and 1750, were among mariners and other seafarers.[16] While farmers and those engaged in less risky occupations lived longer, mariners faced more precarious chances for a long life.[17]

Young mariners were the most vulnerable to an early death at sea. Between 1761 and 1800, 50 percent of the mariners died between the ages of twenty and thirty-nine years; as mariners grew older, they were less likely to appear in the probate records at all. Possibly they shifted occupations; but perhaps they died at early ages. The exact opposite pattern obtained for gentlemen and farmers. These men were more likely to die at advanced ages, over sixty years. These very same patterns of the age at death by occupational groups also occurred during the early eighteenth and nineteenth centuries. While Beverly's mortality experiences selected out those in high-risk occupations, most men in Wenham were farmers or gentlemen. As a rule, they died over the age of sixty years; the few artisans or mariners who lived in Wenham died well under the age of sixty.[18]

The people of Beverly and Wenham saw their populations change for somewhat different reasons. Young mariners in Beverly died, resulting in a higher turnover of the population as a result of mortality, while in Wenham, out-migration caused the population to shift more readily than mortality. From one point of view, Wenham was a "healthier" town than the seaport of Beverly. But the village was persistently overcrowded; migration, not mortality, reduced the size of its population. In nearby Beverly, deaths among males, especially mariners, combined with out-migration to permit continued population growth and turnover.

CHAPTER 3

POPULATION TURNOVER AND ECONOMIC PROSPECTS

DURING THE eighteenth century, the dynamics of population growth altered the patterns of mobility in Beverly and Wenham. Stability and permanence, the desired ideals of the people of the New England town, were no longer assured. Small, farming towns throughout eastern Massachusetts witnessed the migration of their people to western Massachusetts and to New Hampshire and Maine, the "eastern frontier." In seaports like Beverly, though, migrants came and went as people searched for work. Neither Beverly nor Wenham was a self-contained town, hermetically sealed off from the rest of society; two newcomers entered each town for every three matured sons who became taxpayers. In the transitional demographic regime of the mid-eighteenth century, both newcomers and native sons sought out scarce economic resources. One group remained in Beverly or Wenham; another moved to the "eastern frontier" or to a commercial port; and still another became part of a floating population, transients who moved from town to town, searching for work, but never finding a secure niche in society. It was these three groups—permanent residents, migrants, and transients—that had to adjust to the changing social, demographic, and economic life of eighteenth-century Massachusetts.

Recent studies of the New England town during the eighteenth century have depicted a "world of scarcity" in which "overcrowding" was more common than not.[1] Migration, in particular, is viewed as symptomatic of the economic decline of the New England town in the decades before the Revolution. But we need to understand the implications of migration more fully: what were the effects of population growth and land scarcity on different groups of people not only in farming towns like Wenham but also in the emerging seaports like Beverly? This chapter compares the level of entry on the economic ladder of those people who became permanent residents, migrants, and transients. How well these groups fared over time will be discussed in a subsequent chapter. Only by examining the people who moved, as well as those who did not, can one assess the relative impact of population growth and migration on the people of Beverly and Wenham.

THE DISTRIBUTION OF ECONOMIC PROSPECTS

Our knowledge of the economic prospects of migrants and nonmigrants in America is predicated, to a large degree, on the research of historians and sociologists who have studied nineteenth- and twentieth-century urban life. It is agreed that foreign immigrants generally ranked lower on the occupational ladder than native Yankees; that some immigrant groups improved their economic status over time, moving up the "escalator" while other groups took their more menial jobs; that some nineteenth-century urban migrants, particularly blacks, ranked lower and advanced less than either immigrants or Yankees; and that among the three groups in the modern metropolis—the nonmigrants, the native migrants, and the immigrants—the native migrants, at least during the twentieth century, found more jobs open than either immigrants or blacks. Historically, two models best explain the sequential development of the entry level of newcomers to the city. During the nineteenth century, foreign immigrants entered at the bottom of the economic ladder but moved up the "urban escalator" as newer immigrants took their places at the bottom. But in the twentieth century, native Yankee migrants to the city ranked higher than those who were already there; the permanent residents no longer represented the group with the most advantageous economic position.[2]

When considering the economic prospects of migrants and nonmigrants in eighteenth-century America, two facts are critical. First, migration into Beverly or Wenham was not nearly as high as in-migration to the nineteenth-century city. Population growth occurred primarily from within, not from without. Second, the occupational structure of these towns was vastly simpler than the modern metropolis; the sheer existence of fewer jobs meant that occupational advancement was less possible than it would be later. Still, the models of how migrants fit into the economic structure of the industrial city are useful as a basis of comparison. The eighteenth-century experience, at least for these two Massachusetts communities, was not unitary. Migrants and nonmigrants alike found better economic prospects in Beverly than in Wenham; even in preindustrial America, larger, more occupationally diverse towns offered more attractions to migrants. But the village of Wenham was hard pressed to attract permanent migrants. Indeed, it was not always able to sustain its native sons. Access to wealth depended both on what type of town one chose to enter as well as one's status as a migrant. Some migrants did well in Beverly, while this was less true for those in Wenham. Generally, though, permanent residents fared better than migrants in both towns.

The initial task is to assess the relative permanence of both matured sons and newcomers in Beverly and Wenham. It was from these two parts of the population that the stable members of each community came, together with their wives and children. Length of residence may be defined in many ways, from the number of residential moves per year to those per lifetime. In this instance, length of residence represented the number of appearances of resident, male taxpayers on the provincial tax lists, calculated at ten-year intervals. Those who appeared once were migrants; those who persisted on two or more lists were continuous residents. As imperfect as these definitions of residence may be, they permit a systematic gauge of the level of stability. In the cases of Beverly and Wenham, they reveal remarkable similarities in the continuity of matured sons in both towns. About two-thirds of the native sons who first appeared on the tax lists became permanent residents (see Table 3–1). This continuity of matured sons confirms the basic demographic component of population growth in early America: growth from within. Moreover, with native sons remaining in each town at such high rates, cultural continuity passed naturally from generation to generation.

TABLE 3–1. *Length of Residence by Migrant Status in Beverly and in Wenham, 1731–1771*

	New Taxpayers		Disappearing Taxpayers	
Length of Residence	Matured Sons	In-migrants	Deaths	Out-migrants
Beverly 1741–1771				
Short-term	38%	65%	40%	70%
Long-term	62%	35%	60%	30%
N	(295)	(200)	(291)	(284)
Wenham 1731–1771				
Short-term	34%	70%	17%	76%
Long-term	66%	30%	83%	24%
N	(118)	(66)	(108)	(107)

SOURCES: Beverly and Wenham tax lists and reconstitution data.

NOTE: The data from Beverly and Wenham have been collapsed into one aggregate for each town. For Beverly, these data include the period 1741–1771, with taxpayers drawn from decennial tax lists. In Wenham, this aggregate includes the period 1731–1771, also drawn decennially. One-time appearances for taxpayers who were listed only in 1771 are not included in this table or elsewhere in this analysis.

All tables which include only data from Beverly and Wenham will be presented in this aggregated form unless otherwise indicated by decennial tax list years.

In contrast, newcomers were a more mobile group, particularly those in Wenham. About two-thirds of all newcomers were short-term residents, staying long enough to be taxed at least once and then moving on. Compared with matured sons, newcomers were almost twice as likely to migrate. This transiency reveals why many newcomers did not contribute to the growth of the towns.

Permanence in a community, whether for a maturing son or for a migrant, depended largely on access to economic resources, and during the eighteenth century, the commercial town of Beverly was more attractive to newcomers than was Wenham. With its declining land supply and growing population, the trickle of migrants who entered Wenham tended to be relatively poor. Newcomers to Beverly, however, consistently ranked high on the economic ladder in all three wealth categories (see Table 3–2). Compared with matured sons, newcomers to Beverly were almost twice as likely to rank among the wealthiest part of the population. At the middle range of the economic ladder, matured sons and migrants clustered together in a more balanced pattern, particularly with respect to personal property. But at the bottom of the ladder, newcomers were underrepresented as compared with matured sons (50 percent in-migrants vs. 63 percent matured sons). As a group, newcomers to Beverly more closely reflected the actual distribution of wealth of the general population than did matured sons of that town.

By contrast, migrants to Wenham were less well-off. About 70 percent of the newcomers to the village ranked at the bottom of the ladder. On the other hand, maturing sons in Wenham enjoyed a broader access to wealth than did the newcomers. Admittedly, some newcomers in Wenham gained access to substantial property, resulting in a high economic ranking. Such men often migrated to Wenham after living in several other towns first, and then gained land either by purchase or through inheri-

TABLE 3–2. *Wealth Rankings of Matured Sons and In-migrants in Beverly and in Wenham, 1731–1771*

	Real Property		Personal Property	
Wealth Rank at First Appearance	Matured Sons	In-migrants	Matured Sons	In-migrants
Beverly 1741–1771				
Top 20%	9%	16%	8%	16%
Mid 40%	29%	34%	37%	38%
Low 40%	63%	50%	55%	46%
N	(295)	(200)	(295)	(200)
Wenham 1731–1771				
Top 20%	14%	8%	14%	15%
Mid 40%	33%	21%	39%	17%
Low 40%	53%	71%	47%	68%
N	(118)	(66)	(118)	(66)

SOURCE: Beverly and Wenham tax lists and reconstitution data.

NOTE: First appearance is defined as the initial time period when a taxpayer appeared on one of the tax lists which was analyzed; it does not refer to the exact time period of first appearance. However, all taxpayers who entered the very first tax lists analyzed were identified to prevent long-term residents from mistakenly being designated as new persons.

tance. Isaac Dodge, for example, was a cooper in Beverly until 1747, when he moved to Methuen. His wife, Lois Herrick, was a native of Wenham when they married in 1732. While in Methuen, Isaac bought a seventy-acre farm from Benjamin Herrick and moved his large family to Wenham in time to appear on the 1751 tax list. Obviously a restless man, Dodge moved again in 1763, to a new farm in nearby Ipswich Hamlet, after remarrying when his wife died.[3] While the story of Isaac Dodge is interesting and instructive, he was far more successful than others.

Those who moved to small, farming villages like Wenham found a world of scarcity awaiting them, while migrants to

Beverly encountered a world of plenty. In Beverly, newcomers were older, on an average of thirty-six years of age compared with twenty-seven years for native sons in 1761. Just as with Issac Dodge, migrating later in the life cycle permitted some newcomers to have acquired more wealth than native sons just coming of age. Such men as these also had larger families.

Beverly not only attracted newcomers but also accommodated its native sons. Ironically, this equilibrium was achieved, in part, by Beverly's high mortality rate. With jobs often tied to the maritime trade of Beverly and nearby Salem, matured sons and newcomers took up the places of those who died. In a sense, Beverly abated the pressures of population growth both by its commercial economy and by the risks that economy engendered. Newcomers sought out the attractions of Beverly, though their fate was perhaps to be the same as those who had preceded them.

In Wenham, native sons almost dominated access to wealth because economic prospects were defined primarily in terms of land. But only through depopulation could the scarce resources be distributed among the native sons who remained. With a narrow range of occupations in Wenham, migrants almost had to be like Issac Dodge and bring their wealth with them; there was no colonial version of the "escalator" for the migrant to the farming town, as control and distribution of land became of central concern.

After the 1720s, native sons from Wenham and other towns moved to western Massachusetts, New Hampshire, and Maine, as well as to the commercial towns along the seacoast. Well before the urbanization of nineteenth-century America, migrants sought out either the frontier farms or the commercial towns. By the mid-eighteenth century, the demands of the market economy and differential migration—rather than public policy which adjusted town boundaries—corrected the imbalance between population and resources.

THE DIMENSIONS OF OUT-MIGRATION

What happened to these out-migrants after they left Beverly and Wenham is beyond the scope of this inquiry. While tracing each migrant to another town and another job or farm would be an almost impossible chore, we may nevertheless seek to understand how out-migrants fitted within the economic structures of Beverly and Wenham. Our images of migrants in American culture have been drawn primarily from the nineteenth-century, with hopeful young people moving to the western frontier or the city as they beat a path to the upper reaches of society. By contrast, colonial America has been portrayed as a fixed or static society with little geographic mobility. But the evidence from Beverly and Wenham reveals a different picture. Out-migrants from these towns were primarily "repeating" migrants; they were men who had already moved into the towns, and moved again. Economic hardships "pushed" some of them out, while others were "pulled" by the lure of more attractive opportunities elsewhere. The people who remained in Beverly and Wenham were the permanent residents, a core who provided cultural and economic stability.

In his pioneering study of residential mobility, Sidney Goldstein identified similar groups of continuous residents and repeating migrants in Norristown, Pennsylvania, during the twentieth century. Goldstein was struck by what he thought were extremely high rates of repeating migration in Norristown, rates which ranged between 49 and 60 percent from 1930 to 1950.[4] But such rates of repeating migration were not unique to the modern, industrial city. In eighteenth-century Beverly and Wenham, the extent of repeating migration actually surpassed that of Norristown's migrants. In the village of Wenham, repeating migrants entered and left at rates of 67 to 92 percent between 1731 and 1771. In Beverly, repeating migration occurred at about the same level, ranging between 68 and 86 percent (see

TABLE 3–3. *Repeating Migration in Beverly and in Wenham, 1731–1771*

Out-migrant Status and Year of First Appearance	Beverly		Wenham	
	Matured Sons	In-migrants	Matured Sons	In-migrants
1731–1741				
Deaths	—	—	72%	29%
Out-migrants	—	—	28%	71%
N	n.a.	n.a.	(39)	(17)
1741–1751				
Deaths	62%	14%	38%	8%
Out-migrants	38%	86%	62%	92%
N	(84)	(59)	(29)	(13)
1751–1761				
Deaths	52%	32%	59%	20%
Out-migrants	48%	68%	41%	80%
N	(86)	(54)	(22)	(15)
1761–1771				
Deaths	39%	23%	47%	33%
Out-migrants	61%	77%	53%	67%
N	(71)	(70)	(19)	(18)
Total				
Deaths	52%	22%	56%	24%
Out-migrants	48%	78%	44%	76%
N	(241)	(183)	(109)	(63)

SOURCES: Beverly and Wenham tax lists and reconstitution data.
n.a. means not available.

Table 3–3). Overall, three-fourths of the taxpayers who entered Beverly and Wenham also out-migrated.

By comparison, native sons were far more residentially stable than newcomers, with only about one-half out-migrating from either Beverly or Wenham. In Wenham native sons were more likely to out-migrate during the 1740s, and in Beverly, during the 1760s. From the middle decades of the eighteenth century on, the native sons of both village and seaport left town more often but still never as frequently as newcomers. Native sons who inherited property in Beverly and Wenham tended to remain in the towns where they were born. Others simply left.

It was not simply poverty or lack of prospects that compelled people to leave Beverly. Repeating migrants in Beverly clearly ranked in favorable economic positions, particularly those in the top and middle wealth categories (see Table 3–4). Compared with the matured sons of Beverly, newcomers who subsequently out-migrated were surprisingly well-represented in both their real and personal property holdings. To be sure, about one-half of the repeating migrants ranked at the bottom of the economic ladder and were probably "pushed" out of Beverly because of meager economic resources. But those at the top were not forced

TABLE 3–4. *Wealth Rankings at Last Appearance of Out-migrants in Beverly and in Wenham, 1731–1771*

Wealth Rank at Last Appearance[a]	Real Property Out-migrating		Personal Property Out-migrating	
	Matured Sons	In-migrants	Matured Sons	In-migrants
Beverly 1741–1771				
Top 20%	22%	13%	15%	15%
Mid 40%	27%	37%	34%	37%
Low 40%	51%	50%	52%	49%
N	(116)	(142)	(116)	(142)
Wenham 1731–1771				
Top 20%	6%	6%	13%	13%
Mid 40%	44%	19%	33%	19%
Low 40%	50%	75%	54%	67%
N	(48)	(48)	(48)	(48)

SOURCE: Beverly and Wenham tax lists and reconstitution data.

[a] As used in this table, last appearance is defined as the last time period when the taxpayer appeared on a tax list which was analyzed; it does not refer to the exact time period of last appearance.

out; rather, they left, most likely, because of the attractiveness of other towns or jobs, succumbing to the "pull" of new and different economic vistas.

The Wenham migrants were forced to move. Three-fourths of the repeating migrants ranked at the bottom of the real property ladder, while only 6 percent were at the very top. Even in the middle wealth category, newcomers appeared in relatively small proportions, confirming the closed economic structure of Wenham for migrants. This narrow economic structure in Wenham was not limited to repeating migrants, for native sons who out-migrated also ranked in the middle and bottom of the economic ladder.

Rates of persistence among taxpayers, controlled for rank on the economic ladder, reveal that it was the middle and upper classes who provided economic and cultural continuity in Beverly and Wenham (see Table 3–5). If New England towns can be said to have been "peaceable kingdoms," reflecting attitudes of insularity, those attitudes can be directly traced to this group of

TABLE 3–5. *Economic Ranking of Permanent Residents, Percentage of Group at End of Decade*

Decade and Town		Real Property Rank			
		Top 20%	Mid 40%	Low 40%	N
1731–1741	Beverly	n.a.	n.a.	n.a.	n.a.
	Wenham	19%	54%	27%	(67)
1741–1751	Beverly	39%	50%	11%	(151)
	Wenham	27%	49%	24%	(66)
1751–1761	Beverly	41%	48%	11%	(176)
	Wenham	30%	50%	20%	(56)
1761–1771	Beverly	36%	48%	15%	(236)
	Wenham	25%	49%	25%	(59)

SOURCE: Beverly and Wenham tax lists and reconstitution data.
n.a. means not available.

residents who maintained their economic positions. It fell to the floating populations of Beverly and Wenham to make their way in life as best they could, for many were economically marginal. These transients were often dependent on the continuous residents for jobs, social welfare, and charity. The lives of permanent residents and repeating migrants were very much intertwined because transients were employed by permanent residents who also regulated their access to town life.

TRANSIENTS

In discussing the implications of repeating migration which he found in Norristown, Sidney Goldstein suggested that "excessive" migration had serious social and personal implications, perhaps contributing to community instability, diminished family cohesion, and harmful emotional development among the children of migrants.[5] In eighteenth-century Essex County, not all repeating migrants suffered personally; some obviously thrived by frequent moves. Yet a small but growing portion of the repeating migrants were transients, who ranked lowest on the economic ladder.[6] A majority of these transients were single men and women. Most were young, but a few were elderly people who had fallen on hard times and had difficulty qualifying for poor relief.[7] The elderly transients perhaps comprised some 15 percent of the total, while the remainder were single persons and families.[8] Transient families were usually small, averaging about one or two children per family. Younger transients often were ex-servants who sought jobs in a variety of towns, particularly the commercial ports like Beverly, Salem, and Newburyport. As their terms of service ended, they sought new work and moved from place to place, usually not more than ten miles from their last place of residence.[9] Some male transients had served in the army, often in exchange for termination of their servitude. For example, over one-fifth of the privates from Essex County who served in the French and Indian War in

1758 were servants. When their military service ended, they moved. Daniel Buteman from Beverly was one such private, who appeared briefly on the Beverly tax lists, married a local woman, and then left town.[10]

In nearby Salem, transients were employed as artisans, mariners, and laborers.[11] Only a handful could be found in higher-status occupations. These men were often foreigners, nearly two-thirds of whom were mariners or fishermen. Only about one-quarter of the native-born transients were seamen. Whereas similar proportions of both domestic and foreign transients were unskilled workers, far fewer foreign than native-born transients were artisans: tailors, ship's carpenters, or cabinet-makers.

Transient, native-born artisans in Massachusetts should not be confused with English "tramping artisans" of the eighteenth and nineteenth centuries.[12] Migrant artisans in England belonged to a more clearly-defined subculture than did transients in America. Transiency in the towns and seaports of eighteenth-century Essex County, individualized and nonunionized, lacked informal cooperation except among relatives whereas English "tramping" was an organized form of unemployment relief and labor redistribution.

About one-third of all transients in Salem and Boston were European immigrants; in the smaller seaports and the inland towns most transients came from within Massachusetts.[13] Indeed, in small farming villages, transients came almost exclusively from nearby towns. Except for foreign immigrants, the majority of transients entered towns within a ten-mile radius.[14]

Many of the transients who entered farming towns like Wenham were agricultural laborers who worked as hired hands as farmers needed help during the spring planting, summer cultivation, and fall harvest. Richard Dodge, a life-long resident of Wenham, hired Thomas Colwell and his family in 1738. Colwell had migrated to Wenham from New Hampshire and received a small house in which to live. It was not unusual for

	William Vannan Dr	£		
1761 Novbr 4	To a peck of meal	00	01	00
18	To 70 lb of Beef a 2 pr lb	00	11	08
	To 1/2 a Bushel of meal	00	02	00
	To 1/2 a Bushel of meal	00	02	00
	To holling your goods	00	10	00
1762	To Keeping your girl and finding her a peire of Shoes	00	12	00

	Novbr William Vannan Cr			
1761	By a Day at Drilling Stons	00	01	04
	Ditto	00	01	04
	By 1/2 a Day pulling turnops	00	00	08
	By a Day to killing hogs	00	01	04
	By three Days work	00	04	00

Benjamin Haggett Debtor

Benjamin Haggett Credit

August the 10 1786 then Reckoned and settled And Ballanced all accounts with Abner Haggett and the widdow martha Haggett and there is Due To me the sum of Four Pounds thirteen Shillings And five pence As Witness our hands

PLATE 3–1. Pages from the Dodge family account book, showing the work William Vannan performed for Jacob Dodge, and the food and services received in return. Courtesy Wenham Historical Association and Museum, Inc., Wenham, Massachusetts.

Dodge to hire a servant family. Married in 1724, Dodge's wife, Mary, had given birth to seven children by 1738—but only one was alive by the end of that year. Without maturing children in a farming economy, Richard Dodge desperately needed labor to help run his farm.[15]

Other transients were not even wage laborers. William Vannan and his wife moved from Ipswich to Wenham, exchanging his labor for food, clothing, grain, shelter, the use of a house, and shoes for his daughter. Vannan worked for Jacob Dodge, Sr., in 1761 and 1762, and was in town long enough to be taxed, for his wife to give birth to a daughter, and to work for Dodge at drilling stones, pulling turnips, and killing hogs. But he and his family were the targets of local violence—the exact cause is unknown—and he fled (see Plate 3–1).

Many out-migrants, whether they were matured sons or repeating migrants, successfully relocated in other New England farm towns or even in seaports like Boston or Salem. But others were not successful, and in villages and seaports like Beverly and Wenham a class of the migrant poor began to emerge. While some of these transients moved out of menial work as servants, others remained as seasonal agricultural laborers, never able to become the independent yeoman who was the American ideal. Below these laborers were those trapped in a cycle of poverty, dependent on public poor relief and the charity of their neighbors.

CHAPTER 4

ECONOMIC MOBILITY

JACOB DODGE lived in Wenham all of his life, as had his father before him. Jacob was a vigorous man. Marrying his third wife in 1752, he fathered his last child in 1770. In all, Jacob was the father of eleven children, ten of whom survived to adulthood. But Jacob's world did not center only on his numerous children and his prosperous farm. Rather, the world of Jacob Dodge was an extensive one, involving personal and economic ties with his brothers, their families, and the town. Of his four brothers, three—Richard, William, and Skipper—lived in Wenham, having shared in the distribution of their father's land (see Plate 4–1). Only one of Jacob's brothers migrated out of Wenham, moving to Sutton, Massachusetts.[1]

Yet the life patterns of Jacob and his brothers were not to be repeated by their children. Population growth had drained the economic prospects in towns like Wenham, so the Dodge children had to go elsewhere. Richard Hubbard Dodge, Jacob's eldest son, moved on first, joining his uncle in Sutton. The next to leave was Nathaniel Hubbard Dodge, who headed for Hampton Falls, New Hampshire, during the 1760s. Jacob's third-born, Barnabus, was next, going to nearby Gloucester when he married. With his older sons moving out of Wenham, Jacob Dodge had to hire more day laborers to run his farm.

In time, though, his younger sons grew up and two out of the three of them remained in Wenham. William married a woman from Boxford, a small town near Wenham but returned as the

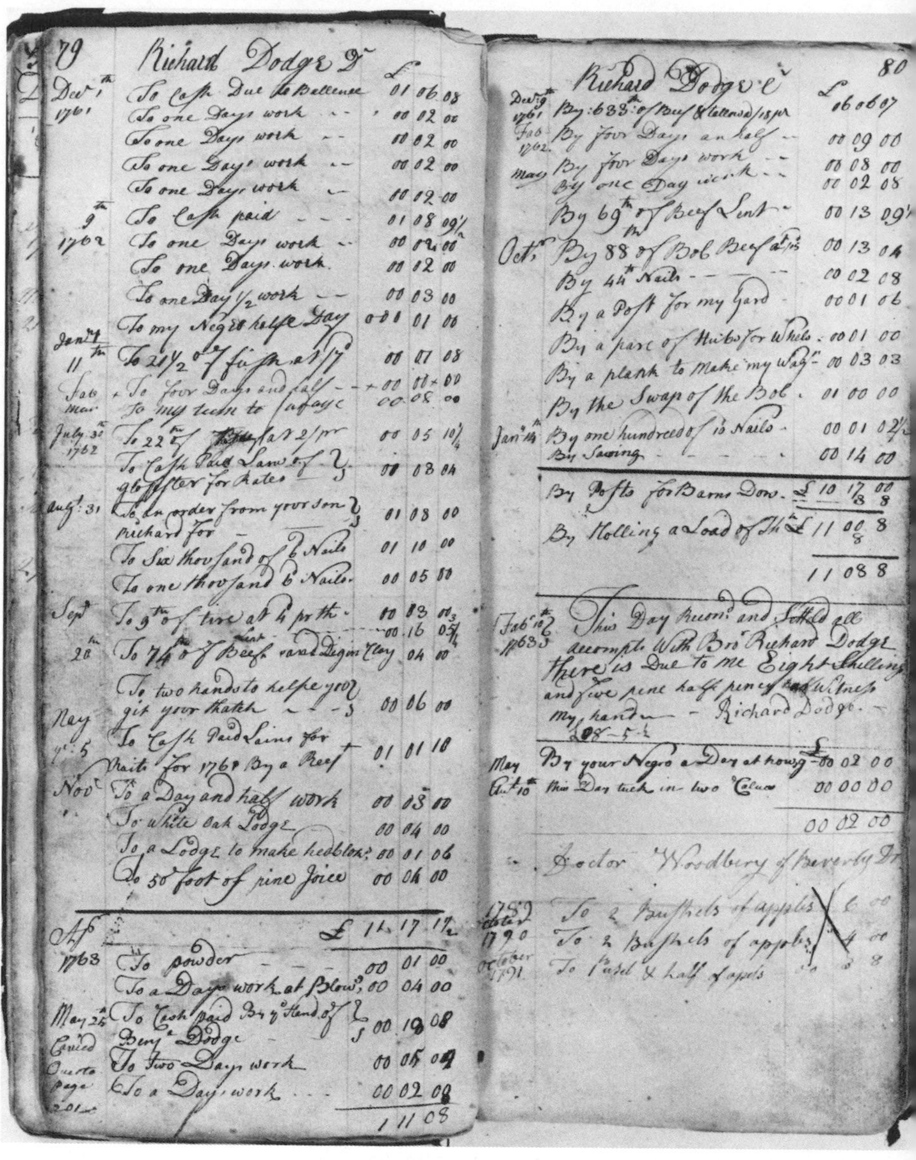

79 Richard Dodge Dr £

Decr 1th 1761 To Cash Due to Ballence 01 06 08
To one Days work 00 02 00
To one Days work 00 02 00
To one Days work 00 02 00
To one Days work 00 02 00
9th To Cash paid 01 08 09½
1762 To one Days work 00 02 00
To one Days work 00 02 00
To one Day ½ work 00 03 00
To my Negro halfe Day 00 01 00
Janry 11th To 21½ of fish at 7 00 07 08
Feb To four Days and half 00 09 00
Mar To my teeme to [illegible] 00 08 00
July 30 1762 To 22th of [illegible] at 2/pr 00 05 10½
To Cash Paid Lamson of Glocester for Rates 00 08 04
Augt 31 To an order from your son Richard for 01 08 00
To Six thousand of 6d Nails 01 10 00
To one thousand 6d Nails 00 05 00
Sept To 9th of [illegible] at 4 pr th 00 03 00
20th To 74th of Beef Lent 00 16 05½
To two hands to helpe your git your thatch 00 06 00
May 5 To Cash Paid Lains for Rates for 1768 By a Reef 01 01 10
Novr To a Day and half work 00 03 00
To white Oak Lodge 00 04 00
To a Lodge to make hedblocks 00 01 06
To 50 foot of pine Joice 00 04 00

£ 11 17 1½

Apl 1763 To powder 00 01 00
To a Days work at Blows 00 04 00
May 25 To Cash paid By ye Hand of Beny Dodge 00 19 08
To two Days work 00 05 00
To a Days work 00 02 00

1 11 08

Richard Dodge Cr 80 £

Decr 9th 1761 By 633th of Beef & tallow at 18 pr 06 06 07
Feb 1762 By four Days an half 00 09 00
May By four Days work 00 08 00
By one Day work 00 02 08
By 69th of Beef Lent 00 13 09½
Octr By 88 of Bob Beef at 1½ 00 13 04
By 4th Nails 00 02 08
By a Post for my Yard 00 01 06
By a pare of [illegible] for Whels 00 01 00
By a plank to Make my Way 00 03 03
By the Swap of the Bob 01 00 00
Janr 14 By one hundred of 10 Nails 00 01 02½
By Sawing 00 14 00

By Posts for Barns Door £ 10 17 8
By Holling a Load of [illegible] £ 11 00 8

11 08 8

Feb 10th 1763 This Day Reckoned and Settled all accompts With Brother Richard Dodge there is Due to me Eight Shillings and five pence half peney as Witness my hand — Richard Dodge
08–5½

May By your Negro a Day at [illegible] 00 02 00
[illegible] 10th this Day tuck in two Calves 00 00 00

00 02 00

Doctor Woodbery of Beverly Dr

1789 October To 2 Bushels of apples
1790 To 2 Bushels of apples
October 1791 To Bushel & half of apples

PLATE 4–1. Pages from the Dodge family account book, illustrating the economic relationship between Jacob Dodge and his brother, Richard. Courtesy Wenham Historical Association and Museum, Inc., Wenham, Massachusetts.

executor of his father's estate. Jacob, Jr., worked with his father during the late 1780s and served in several town offices, but he too moved, to New Boston, New Hampshire. Only Abraham, Jacob's last-born son, never left Wenham. All four of the daughters of Jacob married men who lived outside of Wenham, although only one of them migrated (to New Hampshire). Clearly, the children of Jacob Dodge benefited from growing up in the family of a prosperous and well-respected man. Dodge, who served on numerous town committees, was well-liked by his neighbors. But the close-knit family life developed by Jacob Dodge could not be sustained as his children grew up.

For the eldest sons of Jacob, economic advancement meant out-migration. When Nathaniel was twenty-three years of age, for example, he received an account book that undoubtedly symbolized his growing participation in the family farm. Nathaniel boldly printed his name and the year, 1762, in "His Book." But he never had an opportunity to use that book, for he moved on, relinquishing the book to his father. Jacob remained active until his death in 1793, running his farm and his family as best he could. And the records of that account book, which included entries brought over from the "old book," spanned two generations, dating far back to the 1740s and continuing until Jacob's son, William, settled and "reckoned" all of his father's accounts during the 1790s. With the death of Jacob Dodge, a way of life disappeared. Most of his children sought out economic opportunities beyond the borders of the town, losing the direct continuity of the family farm economy established by their father. Perhaps their own lives were not substantially different from his—they farmed, served on town committees, and raised families—but their roots were no longer in Wenham, where they had been for three generations.

Indeed, the people of Beverly and Wenham became increasingly mobile during the middle of the eighteenth century, as native sons, even newcomers, entered and left the towns in startlingly high proportions. Some left but others remained. Although some newcomers found sufficient economic opportunities to keep them in place for at least a decade, most of those who remained in either Beverly or Wenham were native sons and their families. Beverly offered more chances for economic advancement for both native sons and newcomers than Wenham did. While the patterns of economic mobility appeared to be similar in each of the two towns, particularly in the two decades before the Revolution, economic advancement in Wenham was limited almost entirely to maturing sons while in neighboring Beverly, migrants advanced alongside maturing sons.

The history of economic mobility in eighteenth-century Beverly and Wenham needs to be viewed in a broader perspective. In modern America, newcomers to cities are more economically successful than those who migrate to rural areas.[2] Unlike the western frontier, which Frederick Jackson Turner asserted was the source of economic and social change, the modern metropolis provided the avenues for economic advancement for most migrants in America. With their expanded markets and diverse occupational structures, modern-day cities attracted more migrants than farming towns. But how did migrants fare in the eighteenth-century village of Wenham and the seaport of Beverly?[3] Situated as it was next to Salem, Beverly was a small port within the shadow of one of the major commercial centers of eighteenth-century America. Wenham, on the other hand, faced the problems of depopulation and land scarcity so common to other eastern Massachusetts towns.

PATTERNS OF ECONOMIC MOBILITY

The first concern is to examine the extent of economic mobility during the middle decades of the eighteenth century. In the decades before 1751, the men who entered the economic structures of Beverly and Wenham were less likely to move up the economic ladder and more likely to move down than those who appeared on the tax lists in the two decades before the Revolution. In Wenham, the pressures of land constriction were especially acute during the 1730s. Of the men who first appeared on the tax lists in 1731, only 30 percent moved up the economic ladder within a decade while 21 percent moved down. Stability was more common, as nearly one-half of the men remained in the same place (see Table 4–1). Gradually the economic situation began to improve, chiefly as a result of out-migration. Among the men who appeared on the tax lists in 1741, 48 percent moved up the ladder within ten years, while only 12 percent slipped down. By 1751, economic advancement attained some measure of predictability. Upward mobility became more common than stability for those starting

TABLE 4–1. *Real Property Mobility among Permanent Residents: The First Ten Years*

Decade and Town	Up	Down	Stable	N
1731–1741				
Beverly	—	—	—	n.a.
Wenham	30%	21%	49%	(66)
1741–1751				
Beverly	38%	12%	50%	(136)
Wenham	48%	12%	40%	(65)
1751–1761				
Beverly	54%	9%	38%	(160)
Wenham	57%	4%	39%	(54)
1761–1771				
Beverly	54%	9%	37%	(225)
Wenham	52%	7%	40%	(57)

SOURCES: Beverly and Wenham tax lists and reconstitution data.
n.a. means not available.

NOTE: The mobility matrices from which this table was derived were all significant with the chi square below the 0.001 level.

in 1751 and 1761 as 52 to 57 percent of the men made gains. Only 4 to 7 percent moved down the ladder, while stability eased to 40 percent. By the second half of the eighteenth century, those men who were able to gain access to economic opportunity in Wenham found either upward mobility or stability; few moved down within a decade.

In neighboring Beverly, much the same pattern obtained during the middle decades of the eighteenth century. About half the men who started out in 1741 maintained their economic rank rather than moving up or down. After 1751, upward mobility was as common in Beverly as it was in Wenham: 54 percent of the men made economic gains while about 38 percent remained stable. The men who remained in Beverly and Wenham after 1751 had almost identical patterns of economic mobility during their first ten years of residence.

The twenty-year residents were even more successful. For those men starting on the tax lists in 1731 in Wenham, only 40 percent moved up the economic ladder within 20 years (see Table 4–2). A mere decade later, however, 79 percent of the taxpayers moved up, 21 percent remained stable, and none moved down. This same pattern of upward mobility continued for those starting on the tax lists after 1751. Much the same pattern occurred in Beverly. By 1751, 78 percent of the men in that seaport moved up the economic ladder while only 2 percent moved down.

In Wenham, of course, the migration of maturing sons made possible the upward economic mobility of permanent residents. But in Beverly, the town expanded its boundaries during the 1750s and developed its commercial and maritime economy. With the disruption of the upward movement of sons in Wenham, out-migration was the primary economic alternative. In contrast, Beverly's expanding economy meant that migrants as well as matured sons would advance. A glance at Table 4–3 confirms that a taxpayer's initial economic status was related to

TABLE 4–2. *Real Property Mobility among Permanent Residents: The First Twenty Years*

Decade and Town	Up	Down	Stable	N
1731–1751				
Beverly	—	—	—	n.a.
Wenham	40%	18%	42%	(45)
1741–1761				
Beverly	54%	11%	36%	(95)
Wenham	79%	—	21%	(14)
1751–1771				
Beverly	78%	2%	20%	(54)
Wenham	66%	—	33%	(15)

SOURCES: Beverly and Wenham tax lists and reconstitution data.
n.a. means not available.
NOTE: The measures of chi square significance were as follows: Wenham, 1731–1751, 0.005; Beverly 1741–1761, 0.48; Wenham, 1741–1761, 0.067; Beverly 1751–1771, 0.142; and Wenham, 1751–1771, 0.176.

out-migration. Both matured sons and newcomers who were long-term residents of Beverly and Wenham started their economic lives with distinct advantages over those who appeared only once.

Not all matured sons in Beverly and Wenham found economic advantages, however. The wealthiest matured sons in Beverly were as likely to remain in town as to leave, whereas those in Wenham more often moved on. Matured sons who ranked in the middle of the economic ladder, however, moved in approximately equal numbers in both Beverly and Wenham. But economic disadvantages fell more sharply on those who ranked at the bottom of the ladder, with native sons in both towns appearing briefly as short-term residents and then moving on.

In both Beverly and Wenham, newcomers who persisted were at least twice as likely to rank among the wealthiest tax-

TABLE 4–3. *Real and Personal Property Rankings of Matured Sons and In-migrants in Beverly and in Wenham, by Length of Residence*

Property at First Appearance	Migrant Status and Length of Residence			
	Matured Sons		In-migrants	
	Short-term	Long-term	Short-term	Long-term
Real property				
Top 20%				
Beverly	10%	8%	12%	24%
Wenham	5%	19%	2%	20%
Mid 40%				
Beverly	21%	34%	33%	35%
Wenham	35%	32%	17%	30%
Low 40%				
Beverly	70%	59%	55%	41%
Wenham	60%	49%	80%	50%
N				
Beverly	(112)	(183)	(129)	(71)
Wenham	(40)	(78)	(46)	(20)
Personal Property				
Top 20%				
Beverly	8%	8%	13%	21%
Wenham	11%	18%	12%	25%
Mid 40%				
Beverly	25%	45%	33%	48%
Wenham	32%	41%	16%	20%
Low 40%				
Beverly	67%	48%	54%	31%
Wenham	57%	42%	72%	55%
N				
Beverly	(112)	(183)	(129)	(71)
Wenham	(37)	(74)	(43)	(20)

SOURCES: Beverly and Wenham tax lists and reconstitution data.

payers. Again, in the middle of the economic ladder as many persisted as out-migrated. But four-fifths of the newcomers to Wenham at the bottom of the ladder left town. Propertyless migrants were pushed out of Wenham, while migrants to Beverly fared better.

ECONOMIC ADVANCEMENT: NATIVE SONS AND NEWCOMERS

The people of eighteenth-century Beverly and Wenham were not imbued with the ideology of success as we think of it today. Rather, families improved their economic status when they inherited land from their parents. Access to wealth came slowly, particularly for maturing sons.[4] Superficially, it appears as though maturing sons in both Beverly and Wenham were equally mobile, for their overall intragenerational mobility rates (combined upward and downward movement) were 67 and 66 percent, respectively (see Table 4–4). But almost twice as many maturing sons in Beverly as in Wenham advanced their economic positions within the first ten years (61 percent vs. 33 percent). This strong showing by Beverly's maturing sons is confirmed by the unusually small proportion who moved down the economic ladder, only 6 percent of those holding real property. In contrast to Beverly, where young men advanced up the economic ladder with regularity, in Wenham, many maturing sons declined in their economic rankings because they were unable to acquire land.

Beverly offered more economic advancement to newcomers than Wenham; 41 percent of its newcomers moved up in Beverly, and only 29 percent in Wenham. In fact, newcomers to Beverly made more gains than did maturing sons in Wenham. The gains that newcomers to Beverly made were substantial; few moved down the economic ladder, especially those who were farmers.

About one-third of the native sons in both Beverly and

TABLE 4–4. *Economic Mobility during the First Decade of Residence: Matured Sons Compared with In-migrants, by Length of Residence in Beverly and in Wenham*

Property, Town and Mobility	First Appearance Compared with Second			
	Ten-year Residents		Twenty-year Residents	
	Matured Sons	In-migrants	Matured Sons	In-migrants
Real property				
Up				
Beverly	61%	41%	65%	29%
Wenham	33%	29%	62%	60%
Down				
Beverly	6%	13%	11%	7%
Wenham	33%	14%	4%	—
Static				
Beverly	33%	46%	24%	64%
Wenham	33%	57%	34%	40%
Personal property				
Up				
Beverly	53%	32%	59%	29%
Wenham	40%	21%	49%	60%
Down				
Beverly	17%	41%	12%	21%
Wenham	27%	21%	13%	—
Static				
Beverly	30%	28%	29%	50%
Wenham	33%	57%	38%	40%
Total N				
Beverly	(94)	(54)	(82)	(14)
Wenham	(30)	(14)	(47)	(5)

SOURCES: Beverly and Wenham tax lists and reconstitution data.

NOTE: This table, and the ones that follow in this chapter, employ collapsed cohorts for both Beverly and Wenham. For Beverly, those who appeared 1741–1761 are included together. For Wenham, the cohort includes those who appeared 1731–1761.

Wenham did not change their economic rank. In contrast, newcomers in both towns were more often stable, not moving up or down (46 percent in Beverly and 57 percent in Wenham). Without economic advancement, newcomers were likely to be unable to provide for growing families, forcing them to move on. Still, migrants to Beverly found more upward mobility than those in Wenham, and were less likely to slip back down the economic ladder. Newcomers to Beverly, it seems, entered the seaport and could expect moderate gains or at least maintain their positions. In contrast, Wenham's migrants—as well as her maturing sons—could make no claims to secure economic expectations. Obviously, some people moved into Wenham, like husbands marrying young women of that village, with expectations of land to be gained through marriage. But these people were more the exception than the rule.

Since economic gain often came more slowly than within a single decade, it is also useful to examine economic advancement of native sons and newcomers resident in these towns for at least twenty years (see Table 4–5). During their second decade of residence, as many native sons as newcomers in Beverly advanced up the economic ladder (49 percent vs. 43 percent). In contrast, those in Wenham were less able to make economic gains during the second decade (30 vs. 20 percent). Overall, there was both more upward mobility, or stability, after twenty years in Beverly than in Wenham. If Wenham's farmers changed positions at all, they tended to move down the economic ladder, opening up places for their children. As a result, the possibilities for upward movement were much less in Wenham than in Beverly.

The declining opportunities in Wenham, as compared with the attractive ones in Beverly, affected out-migrants as well. In Beverly, out-migrants who resided for only ten years were more successful during their first decade of residence than those in

TABLE 4–5. *Economic Mobility during the Second Decade of Residence, by Migrant Status*

Property, Town, and Mobility	Second Appearance Compared with Third for Twenty-year Residents			
	Matured Sons	In-migrants	Nonmigrants	Out-migrants
Real property				
Up				
Beverly	49%	43%	36%	52%
Wenham	30%	20%	18%	14%
Down				
Beverly	9%	7%	15%	8%
Wenham	19%	20%	23%	43%
Static				
Beverly	42%	50%	49%	40%
Wenham	51%	60%	58%	43%
Personal property				
Up				
Beverly	28%	29%	28%	24%
Wenham	40%	20%	33%	—
Down				
Beverly	21%	21%	21%	32%
Wenham	19%	20%	22%	43%
Static				
Beverly	51%	50%	52%	44%
Wenham	40%	60%	45%	57%
Total N				
Beverly	(81)	(14)	(87)	(25)
Wenham	(47)	(5)	(60)	(7)

SOURCES: Beverly and Wenham tax lists and reconstitution data.

Wenham (see Table 4–6). Moreover, out-migrants in Beverly were less likely to fall in economic status than those in Wenham, perhaps because they were searching for better opportunities and were not being pushed out. The very fact that twenty-year residents would choose to out-migrate reveals that social

TABLE 4–6. *Economic Mobility during the First Decade of Residence: Nonmigrants Compared with Out-migrants, by Length of Residence in Beverly and in Wenham*

Property, Town, and Mobility	First Appearance Compared with Second			
	Ten-year Residents		Twenty-year Residents	
	Nonmigrants	Out-migrants	Nonmigrants	Out-migrants
Real Property				
Up				
Beverly	39%	53%	47%	60%
Wenham	21%	42%	48%	71%
Down				
Beverly	15%	9%	8%	16%
Wenham	28%	26%	10%	—
Static				
Beverly	46%	39%	45%	24%
Wenham	52%	32%	42%	29%
Personal property				
Up				
Beverly	32%	40%	41%	56%
Wenham	35%	26%	38%	71%
Down				
Beverly	27%	28%	17%	16%
Wenham	21%	32%	15%	—
Static				
Beverly	41%	32%	43%	28%
Wenham	45%	42%	47%	29%
Total N				
Beverly	(74)	(57)	(91)	(25)
Wenham	(29)	(19)	(60)	(7)

SOURCES: Beverly and Wenham tax lists and reconstitution data.

and geographic mobility remained important options for the people of Beverly and Wenham.

It has been common for historians to portray migrants who moved to the colonial frontier as doing so in order to preserve a way of life. For example, migrants to New Hampshire even chose names for their towns like "New Ipswich" and "New Boston." While this study cannot provide definitive answers to the questions of who moved to the frontier and how well they did, some tentative conclusions may be advanced. First, maturing sons and repeating migrants generally were short-term residents, remaining in Beverly and Wenham for brief periods of time and moving on. While some were propertyless, others were attracted by new opportunities. Also, a small but distinct group of long-term residents (people who lived in Beverly and Wenham for ten years or more), sought new opportunities even though they had made gains where they were. While all their reasons for migrating are not known, the economic evidence suggests that people from Beverly and Wenham were both pushed and pulled to new places. Some, particularly those from Wenham, simply had very little chance of advancing, so they moved out. Those from Beverly appear to have been more prone to start over.

In the preindustrial economy of the eighteenth century, seaports offered more opportunities to migrants than did most farming towns. Only if a migrant was willing to move well beyond his immediate town, into New Hampshire or Maine, for example, would the rural economy offer chances for a better life. Still, those who gained the most in Beverly and Wenham were native sons, not migrants, because they inherited property. But access to economic advancement in Beverly and Wenham came only with increased migration; as some native sons left town and as many newcomers generally stayed but a short time and moved again, a core group of maturing sons and a few newcomers was left who secured moderate economic gains.

After 1751, economic stability in Beverly and Wenham came about because of out-migration.

In these two Massachusetts towns, the impact of population growth was checkered. With land scarce, all of the people of the New England towns could not advance economically. The same low rates of economic mobility found in Beverly and Wenham occurred in eighteenth-century Concord and Hingham as well.[5] Even in large ports like Boston and small seaports like Beverly, economic progress was only moderate, and those at both the top and at the bottom of the economic ladder were as likely to move up as to move out.[6] In general, it can be said that for there to be upward movement, there had to be outward movement. And, so it was in Beverly and Wenham.

CHAPTER 5

FAMILY FORMATION AND MIGRATION

DURING the eighteenth century, the patterns of both age at marriage and marital migration changed as population mobility became a primary solution to maintaining an equilibrium between resources and people. While marriage in eighteenth-century Massachusetts did not have the personal strains associated with coming of age, it nevertheless reflected other societal tensions, particularly that of the impingement of a rapidly expanding population on scarce resources.[1] This chapter examines the impact of demographic and economic change on the process of family formation in Beverly and Wenham by focusing on two critical indicators: age at first marriage and marital migration.

AGE AT FIRST MARRIAGE AND MIGRANT STATUS

The general outlines of age at first marriage in colonial New England are clear: women married in their very early twenties and men married during their late twenties.[2] More important, though, the age at first marriage for both men and women changed over the course of the seventeenth and eighteenth centuries. In seventeenth-century New England, the age at first marriage for men ranged between twenty-five and twenty-seven years. In comparison, women's ages fluctuated from a low of about twenty years among the first generation of settlers to about twenty-two years by 1700 (see Table 5–1). This seventeenth-century pattern of high ages for men and low ages for women resulted from an imbalanced sex ratio; single men outnumbered single women by more than three to one among the earliest immigrants.[3] As time passed and more women emigrated, New England women began to marry somewhat later, at about twenty-two years. By contrast, English women married much later, at an average of at least twenty-four years.[4] One of the most important demographic implications of this relatively low age at marriage in New England was an extremely high fertility rate such that an expanding population began to press beyond its resources.

By the early decades of the eighteenth century, the downward trend in age at marriage for men began. Deviating from the high age at marriage pattern, which was common in preindustrial Europe, New England men began to marry as young as age twenty-three by the middle of the eighteenth century. Despite variation from town to town, the same direction of change prevailed: age at first marriage declined for men and rose slightly for women. At first glance, this decline in age at marriage appears to be an anomaly. Logic would have it that in an agrarian society, age at marriage would rise or remain high to limit access to available resources. In fact, this relationship between age at marriage and resources operated during the seventeenth century but changed during the eighteenth century; land pressures became so great that it was no longer a question of balancing families with resources but of deciding who should gain the few opportunities that did exist. In effect, age at marriage reflected the beginning of the end of the old demographic regime, for marriage was becoming more independent of resources.

Looking more closely at husbands and wives in Beverly and Wenham, the slight variations in age at first marriage in these two towns underscore the impact of population growth and available economic resources on family formation. In the small, agricultural village of Wenham, age at marriage for men fol-

TABLE 5–1. *Mean Ages at First Marriage for Men and Women in Selected New England Towns before 1800*

	Birth Cohorts				Marriage Cohorts		
	Cohorts	Men	Women		Cohorts	Men	Women
Plymouth	1600–1625	27.0	20.6	Hingham	pre–1691	27.4	22.0
Colony	1625–1650	26.1	20.2	Dedham	1640–1690	25.5	22.5
	1650–1675	25.4	21.3	Ipswich	1652–1700	27.2	21.1
	1675–1700	24.6	22.3	Wenham	1681–1700	25.0	20.0
Andover	1600–1699	26.7	22.3				
Beverly	1681–1700	25.5	22.6				
Wenham	1661–1680	27.0	21.0				
	1681–1700	25.6	21.6				
Windsor	1640–1649	25.1	19.8				
	1650–1659	25.4	20.6				
	1660–1669	26.4	21.8				
	1670–1679	26.3	23.0				
Andover	1700–1729	27.1	24.5	Beverly	1701–1720	24.6	22.3
	1730–1759	25.3	23.2		1721–1740	23.9	21.4
Beverly	1701–1720	24.6	21.2		1741–1760	24.4	21.8
	1721–1740	24.0	21.8		1761–1780	24.2	22.3
	1741–1760	23.2	21.5	Wenham	1701–1720	24.8	21.1
Wenham	1701–1720	24.3	22.5		1721–1740	25.2	22.7

	1721–1740	23.5	21.5
	1741–1760	22.8	20.6
	1741–1760	23.2	21.4
	1761–1780	23.9	21.7
Hingham	1716–1740	27.0	23.8
	1741–1760	26.0	22.8
	1761–1780	24.6	23.5
	1781–1800	26.4	23.7
Ipswich	1701–1725	26.5	23.6
	1726–1750	24.0	23.0

SOURCES: John Demos, *A Little Commonwealth: Family Life in Plymouth Colony* (New York: Oxford University Press, 1970), 193, Table IV; Philip J. Greven, Jr., *Four Generations: Population, Land, and Family in Colonial Andover, Massachusetts* (Ithaca: Cornell University Press, 1970), 35; 206; 208; Linda Auwers Bissell, "Family, Friends, and Neighbors: Social Interaction In Seventeenth Century Windsor, Connecticut," (Unpublished Ph.D. dissertation, Brandeis University, 1973), 45, Table 6; Daniel Scott Smith, "The Demographic History of Colonial New England," *The Journal of Economic History,* 32 (1972), 177, Table 3, presents the Hingham data; Kenneth A. Lockridge, "The Population of Dedham, Massachusetts, 1636–1736," *Economic History Review,* 19 (1966), 330; Susan L. Norton, "Population Growth in Colonial America: A Study of Ipswich, Massachusetts," *Population Studies,* 25 (1971), 445, Table 6.

lowed the general pattern of decline almost perfectly. In contrast, the decline in Beverly was somewhat less clear-cut, although it did exist. The implication, though, is that commercial economic opportunities muted the impact of population growth on family formation.

In Wenham, the mean age at marriage of the cohorts of men born before 1700 mirrored the high or "European" ages at marriage. By the first half of the eighteenth century, however, Wenham husbands no longer married as at such high ages. For example, men born between 1721 and 1740, married at a mean age of twenty-three-and-a-half years, down from the twenty-seven years for those born between 1661 and 1680 (see Table 5–2). These lower ages at marriage for men in Wenham coincided precisely with an expanding population and increased

TABLE 5–2. *Age at First Marriage of Men in Beverly and in Wenham, by Birth Cohorts 1661–1760*

	Beverly		
Birth Cohorts	Mean	S.D.	N
1661–1680	23.8	4.126	(12)
1681–1700	25.5	4.113	(45)
1701–1720	24.7	4.456	(108)
1721–1740	24.0	4.729	(128)
1741–1760	23.2	2.926	(84)

	Wenham		
Birth Cohorts	Mean	S.D.	N
1661–1680	27.0	5.020	(15)
1681–1700	25.6	4.677	(27)
1701–1720	24.3	3.441	(48)
1721–1740	23.5	3.487	(45)
1741–1760	22.8	1.920	(20)

SOURCES: Beverly and Wenham tax lists and reconstitution data.

rates of out-migration. Migration became Wenham's answer to family limitation, not a continued high age at marriage among men. Indeed, women's ages at marriage during this period remained constant, at about twenty-one to twenty-two years. In Wenham, balancing resources with people meant that fewer families could remain in the town. Since the land supply was not perceived to be sufficient, it no longer mattered if husbands and wives married early or late. Access to land was the critical concern, not limiting the size of families.

In neighboring Beverly, however, the decline in age at marriage for men was not as dramatic as it was in Wenham. With the cohorts of men marrying between 1681 and 1700 and those marrying between 1741 and 1760, the mean age at marriage fell 2.3 years compared with 2.8 years in Wenham (see Table 5–2). Both absolutely and statistically, Wenham's pattern of declining age at marriage for men was stronger than Beverly's.[5] Because of a combination of commercial growth and differential migration, the demographic equilibrium in Beverly was not as altered by population growth as it was in Wenham. Rather, the decline in the age at marriage among men in village and seaport reflects different—but not dramatic—sociodemographic adaptations during the eighteenth century.

The differential effect of population growth on age at marriage among men in Beverly and Wenham occurred most dramatically among nonmigrants and out-migrants. Other factors —length of residence and property rank on the tax list—were simply not instrumental in affecting family formation in village and seaport (see Tables 5–3 and 5–4). Rather, changes in age at marriage among upper- and lower-class men and long- and short-term taxpayers were similar to those in the general population and reflected the long-term change from the seventeenth to the eighteenth century. But nonmigrants and out-migrants deviated from the general trends, particularly in Wenham. In the village, nonmigrants born before 1720 married at an aver-

TABLE 5–3. *Two-way Analysis of Variance of Age at First Marriage of Husbands and Wives in Beverly, 1661–1760*

Characteristics	Birth Cohorts 1661–1720		Birth Cohorts 1721–1760		Effect and F-test Significance	Proportion of Variance
Husbands						
Length of residence						
Short-term	24.7	(55)	23.7	(122)	cohort	
Long-term	24.9	(110)	23.7	(94)	under 0.05	1.5%
Migrant status						
Matured sons	25.9	(66)	23.6	(186)	NS	
In-migrants	24.4	(24)	24.0	(29)		—
Nonmigrants	24.9	(118)	23.1	(58)	cohort	
Out-migrants	24.9	(40)	24.0	(72)	under 0.05	1.9%
Real property rank						
Top 40%	24.1	(74)	23.1	(32)	cohort	
Low 60%	25.3	(90)	23.8	(184)	under 0.05	1.5%
Personal property rank						
Top 40%	24.3	(75)	23.4	(44)	cohort	
Low 60%	25.2	(89)	23.8	(172)	under 0.05	14%
Wives						
Real property rank of husband						
Top 40%	20.8	(41)	20.5	(12)	real	
Low 60%	22.3	(50)	21.9	(102)	under 0.05	2.0%
Personal property rank of husband						
Top 40%	20.5	(40)	21.1	(27)	personal	
Low 60%	22.5	(51)	22.1	(87)	under 0.05	2.8%

SOURCE: Beverly tax lists and reconstitution data.

NOTE: The two-way analysis of variance used in this table is a factorial design based on two independent variables and one dependent variable, age at first marriage. Each of the independent variables in the left-hand column, "Characteristics," was analyzed in relation to the independent variable, "Birth Cohort." The ages at first marriage are reported for each of the two groups of birth cohorts, 1661–1720 and 1721–1760. The next column presents the "effect" of each variable on age at marriage, or, the "interaction effect" of the two independent variables on age at marriage. Also reported in this column is the significance level of the F-test if at the 0.05 level. If not, the designation

"NS" (not significant) is used to show lack of statistical significance. This designation is also used to denote relationships where the total number of cases was too small to warrant their inclusion in the analysis, although the mean ages at marriage are reported. The last column gives the proportion of the variance in mean age at marriage accounted for by the variable with the main effect or the interaction of the two independent variables.

Wealth rankings in this table are those of last appearance of male taxpayers.

TABLE 5–4. *Two-way Analysis of Variance of Age at First Marriage of Husbands and Wives in Wenham, 1661–1760*

Characteristics	Birth Cohorts 1661–1720	Birth Cohorts 1721–1760	Effect and F-test Significance	Proportion of Variance
Husbands				
Length of residence				
Short-term	23.6 (18)	23.6 (40)	cohort	
Long-term	25.5 (72)	22.8 (25)	under 0.05	2.6%
Migrant status				
Matured sons	24.7 (55)	23.2 (51)	NS	
In-migrants	24.8 (11)	23.6 (14)		—
Nonmigrants	26.2 (57)	22.3 (26)	cohort by migrant	
Out-migrants	23.3 (30)	24.6 (25)	under 0.001	9.7%
Real property rank				
Top 40%	24.8 (37)	23.1 (12)	cohort	
Low 60%	25.3 (53)	23.3 (53)	under 0.05	4.2%
Personal property rank				
Top 40%	25.3 (39)	22.3 (14)	cohort	
Low 60%	25.0 (51)	23.5 (51)	under 0.01	6.2%
Wives				
Real property rank of husband				
Top 40%	21.6 (14)	21.4 (7)	NS	
Low 60%	22.3 (25)	21.3 (28)		—
Personal property rank of husband				
Top 40%	19.8 (13)	21.4 (9)	NS	
Low 60%	23.2 (26)	21.2 (26)		—

SOURCE: Wenham tax lists and reconstitution data.

NOTE: See Note to Table 5–3.

age of 26.2 years, deferring marriage in order to gain access to land. In contrast, the pre-1720 out-migrants married at much younger ages, about 23 years. Clearly, those who knew they could not remain in Wenham—or chose not to remain—married more quickly and moved on. But as the old demographic regime began to weaken in the eighteenth century, nonmigrants born after 1720 reversed the pattern and married very early, at 22.3 years. But out-migrants from Wenham actually delayed their marriages to an average of 24.6 years, perhaps in the hope that they, too, could gain land. But the pressures on land were too great, and so they moved on. By the middle decades of the eighteenth century, marital age was much higher for out-migrants than nonmigrants in Wenham. In contrast, out-migrants in Beverly married at about the same age as nonmigrants.

Age at marriage in Beverly and Wenham was largely dependent on economic resources. In all but one of the tax lists analyzed between 1731 and 1771, between one-fourth and one-third of the maturing sons became taxpayers before they were actually married. Access to wealth did not coincide exactly with marriage for all native sons. The single exception occurred in Wenham in 1741, a year which represented the very height of the population pressures in that town. Over 90 percent of the matured sons who appeared for the first time on the 1741 tax list were married. And more generally, in Wenham most property was in the hands of married men whereas in Beverly single men also shared in the wealth. In 1741, for example, only 47 percent of the matured sons listed for the first time on the tax rolls in Beverly were married.[6]

The sons of wealthier merchants and farmers in Beverly had their choice of brides, and such men tended to marry younger women. The average age at marriage of women whose husbands ranked in the top-fortieth wealth percentile for real property was just over twenty years during both the seventeenth and the eighteenth centuries. In contrast, the age at marriage for women in Wenham during the eighteenth century did not vary by the economic rank of the husband. These differences, however, are not unexpected. Lower-class women married later because they often worked as maidservants for a specified term of years. Elizabeth Nicholson Stimpson, for one, married when she was twenty-four years old, after completing a term of service in various Essex County towns.[7] Conversely, younger, wealthy women were more attractive to potential husbands. Economic status, then, was a boundary that defined family formation more distinctly in Beverly than in Wenham.

The problem was not simply who one married but whether one married at all. During the eighteenth century, a highly unbalanced sex ratio prevailed in Essex County towns, particularly in those towns surrounding Beverly and Wenham. The towns contiguous to Beverly and Wenham had adult sex ratios that ranged from 72 to 90 males for every 100 females in 1765; the overall county sex ratio was only 84. To compound the problem for the people of Beverly and Wenham, the sex ratios of these two towns were the lowest of any other towns in Essex County, 74 and 72, respectively.[8] With out-migration reducing the number of potential husbands, women undoubtedly worried about finding husbands in these eighteenth-century Essex County towns. In nearby Haverhill, Mary Orne Tucker feared that she would be the only unmarried woman among her friends and quite alone. To her relief, she soon married a man from Salem.[9]

Then again, widows also sought husbands, especially younger women who had lost their husbands to the maritime trade or simply an early death. In Beverly, for example, there were seven widows for every widower, hardly suggesting that the odds were in their favor. In fact, younger widows tended to remarry more frequently, and in Beverly, widowers who did remarry usually did so within three years of the death of their first wife.[10] With an imbalanced sex ratio and a strong desire for marriage and remarriage, the men and women of Beverly and Wenham naturally sought out mates, as Mary Orne Tucker did, in neighboring towns.

MARITAL MIGRATION

In 1724, Richard Dodge, a native of Wenham and brother of Jacob Dodge, married Mary Thorne of Ipswich. The couple settled in Richard's hometown, as was the prevailing custom. Technically, Mary "migrated" as a bride from Ipswich to Wenham, but in this instance migration is a deceptive word. Wenham and Ipswich were contiguous towns (and remain so today), so that Mary Thorne moved only a few miles to her new home, while Richard Dodge found his wife only a short distance away.[11] The marriage of Richard and Mary Dodge was not unusual; most of the brides and grooms in Beverly and Wenham selected mates from the same or nearby towns. The geographic boundaries of marital migration—and the social networks of friendships and kinship they imply—meant that for much of the eighteenth century, social interactions extended beyond the borders, but not much further, of the New England town. But with the impact of a growing population, differential migration, and an imbalanced sex ratio, the net of selection stretched wider.[12]

Throughout the eighteenth century, husbands and wives from Beverly were almost three times more likely to have found their mates from within the same town as were their counterparts in Wenham.[13] In Wenham, husbands and wives normally found their partners outside of the town. William Cleaves of Beverly and Joanna Coy of Wenham, who were married in 1747, were but one of numerous couples with one or both spouses from outside of their own towns. But for Joanna, it was more expected to seek a mate from a nearby town than it was for William. In fact, Joanna's father, Caleb

FIGURE 5–1. Marital Endogamy in Beverly and Wenham, by Marital Cohorts, 1681–1840

Coy, traveled to nearby Lynn to marry his bride some thirty years earlier. It was this dynamic pattern of marital migration in Wenham that sharply distinguished it from Beverly; between 1681 and 1840, the rate of marital endogamy in Wenham rose above 50 percent for only one cohort of marital partners, and ranged between 23 and 51 percent (see Figure 5–1). On the other hand Beverly's rate of endogamy fell below 50 percent only once—to 39 percent—and more commonly ranged between 62 and 81 percent.[14]

In marital choices, Beverly residents were less cosmopolitan than Wenhamites. Considering only the extent of marital migration, Beverly was a more insular town, but we must also examine how population size and the extent of population turnover contributed to marital endogamy. With a limited supply of potential marital partners as a result of a relatively small population—diminished even more by a declining population and an imbalanced sex ratio—Wenham's young people had to search beyond their town's borders for marital partners. In contrast, Beverly, with a population almost four times as large as Wenham's, had many more eligible young people. Put more simply, young adults in Beverly were more likely to meet a potential spouse from within their own town than were young people in Wenham.[15]

Population turnover, in addition, increased in Beverly during the eighteenth century, constantly reshuffling the supply of potential husbands and wives. In Wenham, however, the pool of marital partners changed more slowly because of the combined effect of high out-migration and low in-migration. As families moved on, died out, and intermarried, surnames disappeared from the records of the towns. New families, though, entered and replaced those who disappeared. More new surnames appeared on the tax list of 1771 in Beverly than in Wenham, indicating a higher level of population turnover (56 percent in Beverly compared with 44 percent in Wenham). This influx of new families into Beverly occurred even though old families persisted more often in Beverly than in Wenham between 1741 and 1771 (66 percent of surnames appeared twice in Beverly compared with 51 percent in Wenham). Population turnover, particularly in-migration, continuously expanded the number of marital partners in Beverly, while in Wenham the number declined during the eighteenth century. Depopulation in Wenham forced young people to seek partners outside of the town, while in Beverly young people found partners as migrants entered the town.

With a lower rate of marital endogamy than in Beverly, Wenham's system of marriage, at least among migrant marital partners, could best be described as patrifocal: wives generally moved to their husbands' place of residence. This conclusion is substantiated by an analysis of the marriages of residentially stable taxpayers and their wives, which reveals the actual volume of migration of nonresident brides and grooms in village and seaport. Brides in both towns were more than twice as likely as grooms to move, confirming the patrifocal arrangements associated with marriage. More important, among taxpayers, migrant wives and husbands were much more common in Wenham than in Beverly. Because of depopulation, young women in Wenham, like Joanna Coy, had to seek partners from outside of town. The only disruption of this pattern came during the 1730s and 1740s when population pressure was particularly severe. Among the cohort of taxpayers marrying between 1721 and 1740, only 8 percent of the husbands were migrants, compared with 19 percent in the cohort marrying during the previous twenty years. After 1741, higher proportions of migrant husbands returned. Still, it was wives, rather than husbands, who were the typical migrants at marriage during most of the eighteenth century, a pattern that began to change, at least in Beverly, after 1780 (see Table 5–5).

Before 1780, almost all migrant marital partners in both village and seaport came from other towns within Essex County

TABLE 5–5. *Residential Origins at Marriage of Taxpayers and Their Wives in Beverly and in Wenham, 1701–1780*

	Beverly				
Marriage Cohorts	Both Residents	Migrant Husbands	Migrant Wives	Both Nonresidents	N
1701–1720	64%	—	27%	9%	(33)
1721–1740	52%	9%	27%	12%	(77)
1741–1760	58%	12%	25%	5%	(107)
1761–1780	62%	12%	25%	1%	(99)

	Wenham				
Marriage Cohorts	Both Residents	Migrant Husbands	Migrant Wives	Both Nonresidents	N
1701–1720	37%	19%	37%	7%	(27)
1721–1740	48%	8%	39%	5%	(61)
1741–1760	45%	17%	22%	16%	(58)
1761–1780	44%	15%	35%	6%	(34)

SOURCES: For Beverly, calculated from Beverly tax lists and reconstitution data; for Wenham, calculated from Wenham tax lists and reconstitution data.

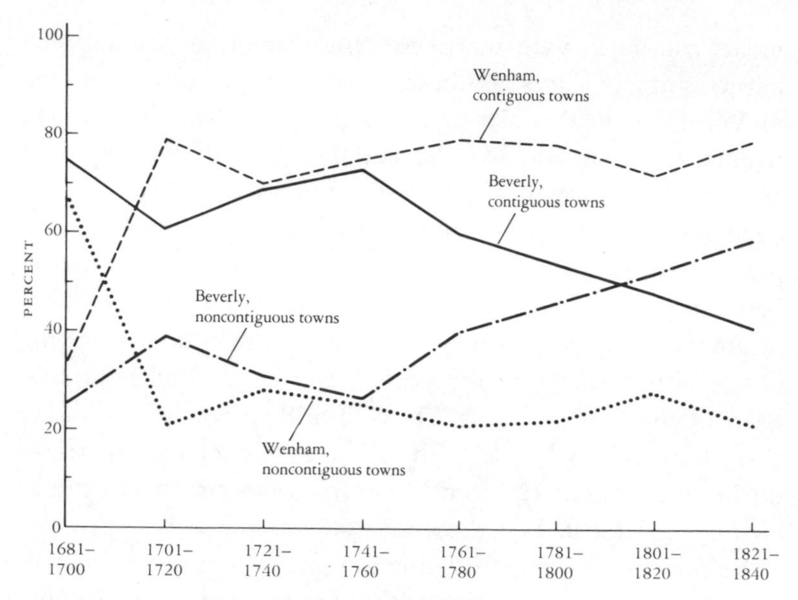

FIGURE 5–2. Residential Origins of Migrant Husbands in Beverly and Wenham, 1681–1840

FIGURE 5–3. Residential Origins of Migrant Wives in Beverly and Wenham, 1681–1840

(see Figures 5–2 and 5–3). In fact, the origins of marital partners were even more geographically confined than within the county; most nonresident spouses came from one of the towns directly contiguous to Beverly or Wenham—Salem, Ipswich, Manchester, Danvers, and Topsfield. When young men and women sought marital partners, they usually went just outside of their own towns of residence, especially those in Wenham. Still, before 1780, most mates selected partners who were born within a few miles of them. This localism of marital networks among the towns contiguous to Beverly and Wenham held true for both men and women, although migrant spouses from outside of Essex County were more often husbands than wives. But after 1780, the women of Beverly began to marry men from elsewhere.[16] The proportions of migrant husbands marrying in Beverly increased after 1780, from 46 to 59 percent. The percentage of migrant husbands who came from outside of Essex County also sharply increased from what it had been before 1780. Long distance migration for marriage was less evident in Wenham than in Beverly. More removed from the major lines of transportation, Wenham's young people were less exposed to the newcomers found in Beverly. As a result, their localistic networks of marriage remained intact after 1780, and the young people of Wenham continued to marry spouses from the contiguous towns.[17]

Well before industrialization and urbanization, the economic and demographic dislocations of the eighteenth century began to alter the patterns of marital age in Beverly and Wenham. Some men married earlier, accelerating the passage to adulthood; others postponed marriage, gathering sufficient economic resources for their future families; and still others gained access to land without marrying. Especially in Beverly, young, marriageable men moved to town. But in Wenham, men and women continued to seek their partners from nearby towns, as the tradition of selecting one's mate locally persisted in the village.

CHAPTER 6

INHERITANCE

DURING the mid-eighteenth century, both migration and economic mobility adjusted the economic resources available to native sons and newcomers in Beverly and Wenham. Many men and their families moved up the economic ladder; some were pushed out by marginal economic opportunities; and still others were pulled elsewhere by the lure of either new lands in New Hampshire or life in a commercial town like Boston. In general, economic success was greater for native sons than migrants. With a growing population and a limited land supply in eastern Massachusetts, not only did young people have to look beyond their towns for marital partners but townsmen in Beverly and Wenham were no longer able to provide additional, open land for the younger generations. The result was that migration to the frontier or to commercial centers absorbed the excess. Fathers were no longer able to pass on land to their sons or settle them in nearby towns, and inheritance practices changed. Even the law of partible inheritance, which has been viewed by many legal historians as the panacea for a wide distribution of wealth in early America, had a minimal impact on the allocation of resources in Beverly and Wenham. Rather, economic constriction slowly modified the ways in which parents passed on their wealth to their children.

INHERITANCE AND INTESTACY: OVERALL PATTERNS

Historians of early New England have traditionally emphasized the importance of inheritance in gaining access to economic resources. The passing on of land from parents to children, and especially from fathers to sons, represented the primary economic and familial relationships between the generations, which provided access to economic opportunity.[1] A father's ownership of property was the material authority in this preindustrial world of the eighteenth century. But studying this transmission of property is not simply a matter of examining wills and practices of inheritance. First, not all men in either Beverly or Wenham died leaving wills, suggesting that parents divided their wealth with deeds of gift before their deaths or left that important decision to the probate courts through the law of intestacy. Second, some men gained their property outside of the inheritance system by learning a trade.

Artisans, mariners, apprentices, and laborers sought skills and jobs rather than land. Mariners, beginning as young boys, served what amounted to an apprenticeship. Josiah Batchellor, III, sailed from Beverly, for example, with the blessings of his father, himself a trader and master of a vessel. Young Josiah was not simply encouraged at a young age to learn the skills of the mariner; his father explicitly helped to provide them.[2] On the schooner *Dolphin* sailing out of Beverly's harbor in 1764 to Virginia were four young men from the town—Ellinwood, Trask, Knowlton, and Foster.[3] Apprenticeships helped these boys secure jobs as adults.[4]

Helping to find a good apprenticeship was one of the more common ways a father assisted his son. It was far less common for a father to pass on property.[5] The evidence from the probate records is startling: of the men who had estates probated in Beverly, only 29 percent had made wills. In Wenham, the proportion was higher (46 percent). The few women in either town who left estates generally left wills (41 percent in Beverly and 65 percent in Wenham). (See Table 6–1.)

But the overall patterns of those who left wills can be a deceptive measure, given the pressures of population growth and land scarcity. During the mid-eighteenth century, men became increasingly concerned with writing wills. With the cohort of men dying 1681–1720, 26 percent in Beverly and 42 percent in Wenham left wills. Between 1721 and 1800, about a third of the men dying in Beverly and one-half of those dying in Wenham left wills. The men in Wenham were consistently more property-conscious than the men in Beverly. Even so, men in

TABLE 6–1. *Percentages of Men and Women Who Died Leaving Wills in Beverly and in Wenham, 1681–1840*

Town	1681–1720	1721–1760	1761–1800	1801–1840	Total
	Men				
Beverly					
Wills	26%	36%	35%	24%	29%
No wills	74%	64%	66%	76%	71%
N	(96)	(216)	(281)	(501)	(1094)
Wenham					
Wills	42%	50%	51%	39%	46%
No wills	58%	50%	49%	61%	54%
N	(24)	(48)	(53)	(49)	(174)
	Women				
Beverly					
Wills	50%	46%	48%	36%	41%
No wills	50%	54%	52%	64%	59%
N	(8)	(26)	(71)	(132)	(237)
Wenham					
Wills	—	50%	80%	67%	65%
No wills	100%	50%	20%	33%	35%
N	(1)	(8)	(10)	(12)	(31)

SOURCE: Essex County Probate Docket, Essex County Court House, Salem, Mass.

both towns during the eighteenth century experienced a heightened concern with the transmission of property to their children. Only after 1800 did the proportions of men leaving wills decline in both towns (24 percent in Beverly and 39 percent in Wenham). Migration played an important part in this shift, for young adults were no longer bound to the world of their fathers by economic ties.

GAINING ACCESS TO LAND

As the supply of land declined while the population continued to rise, the allocation of resources became an increasing problem. Of course, the people of seventeenth-century Beverly and Wenham, as well as people of other Essex County communities like Andover and Salem, also confronted the problem of land scarcity. The seventeenth-century resolutions, however, often involved changes in land titles, town boundaries, and the partitioning of common land.[6] By the early eighteenth century, land issues were more distributional—would there be enough land? The leader of the Massachusetts Bay Colony, John Winthrop, anticipated the possibility of population pressure and the need for additional lands for future generations and hoped that the large town grants could accommodate both maturing children and servants.[7] They did for about one hundred years, but after the 1720s, migration was the primary means of resolving the land crisis in eastern Massachusetts.

The impact of population pressure and a declining land supply on the distribution of property in eastern Massachusetts may be seen most vividly by analyzing the proportions of men who left wills in each decade. As Figure 6–1 illustrates, the patterns of willmaking in both Beverly and Wenham fluctuated sharply during the eighteenth century. In both Beverly and Wenham, willmaking declined dramatically during the decade 1710–1719, when the townspeople of both village and seaport divided their remaining common lands.[8] This action helped to relieve the

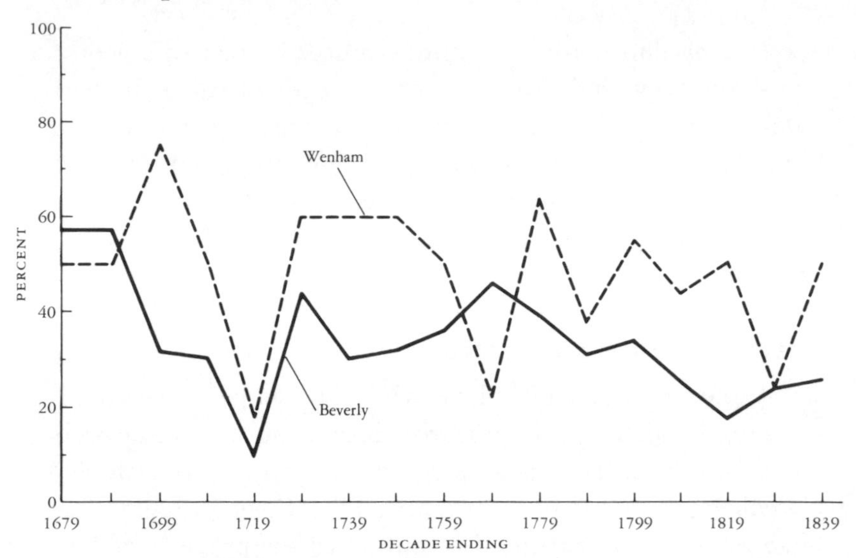

FIGURE 6–1. Proportions of Men Who Died Leaving Wills in Beverly and Wenham, 1679–1839

pressures of land scarcity. Maturing children settled on this land, and townsmen traded it among themselves, perhaps securing capital to purchase land elsewhere. Since families could simply distribute land by gift, they had less need for wills which allocated property. In Wenham, the selectmen had used the common lands as a sort of "bank" upon which they could draw in order to finance the taking of private property for public roads and even to reimburse townspeople for services such as caring for the poor. Other residents, however, began to seek a division of the lands among the townspeople. Only one year before the division in Wenham, a group of residents charged the selectmen—who were selling off common lands to pay town debts—with improper financial management. Although the selectmen were cleared of any impropriety by the General Court, the townspeople decided to divide the land the next year, clearly suggesting that economic pressures resulted in intratown political conflicts.[9]

By the 1720s, a higher proportion of men in both Beverly and Wenham began to make wills. In Wenham, the increase was particularly sharp, with the proportion of men writing wills remaining at 50 to 60 percent until the Revolution, except during the French and Indian War when war-time deaths raised the proportions of intestate men. During the 1720s, the selectmen of Wenham petitioned the General Court to obtain more land by either expanding its town boundaries (hardly feasible) or by allocating unsettled frontier lands to the town. The General Court rejected this plea and the important policy implications it symbolized. Younger generations could no longer rely on town fathers or provincial leaders to expand their economic prospects with new lands.[10] Rather, the patterns of inheritance became even more important as parents attempted to distribute their resources to their children. Family decisions and not town policies became the underpinning of the eighteenth-century response to population growth and land scarcity, particularly in Wenham. In Beverly, there was a decline in willmaking from 1760 to 1840, because so many of the men of the town were seamen who rarely left wills.

THE SOCIAL STRUCTURE OF INHERITANCE AND INTESTACY

Men who chose to make wills, we might presume, were more conscious of the need to make strict provisions for their maturing children than men were who died intestate. Additionally, as some historians have suggested, parents also had to plan for their own old age, and ensure that at least one child remained to care for them. Yet men who left wills tended to be older and wealthier. It is generally true in early New England communities, and in Beverly and Wenham, that older, wealthier people left wills, while young adults (just beginning to build their estates) simply did not write wills because they were not contemplating death.[11] Men who died with wills in Beverly and Wenham were, on average, at least ten years older than those who died intestate (see Tables 6–2 and 6–3), except for the men dying in Beverly between 1700 and 1749, who were on average only six years older than intestate men. Still, the mean age at death among men with wills was substantially higher throughout the eighteenth century and even into the early nineteenth century.

The mean age of death was closely related to a man's occupation. In Beverly, mariners died at the youngest mean ages,

TABLE 6–2. *Mean Age at Death among Male Decedents in Beverly, by Occupation and Testate Status, 1700–1840*

Decedents	Mean Age at Death		
	1700–1749	1750–1799	1800–1840
Males	60.5 (39)	60.7 (152)	55.4 (298)
Occupation			
Gentlemen, professionals, and traders	48.3 (4)	66.7 (28)	58.7 (64)
Shipping and mariners	46.1 (7)	50.6 (31)	43.7 (101)
Artisans	63.8 (10)	55.2 (35)	55.7 (60)
Yeomen and husbandmen	66.9 (18)	66.4 (58)	68.9 (73)
Testate	63.7 (17)	66.0 (82)	64.8 (90)
Intestate	58.0 (22)	54.4 (70)	51.3 (208)

SOURCE: Essex County Probate Docket and Beverly and Wenham tax lists and reconstitution data.

NOTE: The analysis of variance used in Tables 6–2 and 6–3 is a factorial design based on two independent variables and one dependent variable, age at death. Each of the independent variables in the left-hand column, "Decedents," was analyzed in relation to the dependent variable for the three time periods.

For the Beverly decedents, the main effect of the relationship between occupation and mean age at death was statistically significant below the 0.05 level for each of the three time periods. On the testacy variable, the significance level in Beverly for the period 1700–1749 was 0.776, and under 0.000 for the remaining two time periods.

The results in Wenham were not as statistically strong. The main effects between occupation and mean age at death, by time period in Wenham was the following: 1700–1749, 0.666; 1750–1799, 0.285; and 1800–1840, 0.174. On the testacy variable, the significance levels were 0.205 for 1700–1749; 0.189 for 1750–1799; and 0.086 for 1800–1840.

TABLE 6–3. *Mean Age at Death among Male Decedents in Wenham, by Occupation and Testate Status, 1700–1840*

Mean Age at Death	1700–1749		1750–1799		1800–1840	
Male decedents	58.2	(11)	63.9	(29)	62.4	(39)
Gentlemen, professionals, and traders	59.8	(5)	59.1	(11)	60.3	(21)
Shipping and mariners	—	(0)	57.0	(1)	—	(0)
Artisans	49.0	(1)	50.8	(5)	35.0	(1)
Yeomen and husbandmen	58.4	(5)	74.3	(12)	66.5	(17)
Testate	62.7	(7)	69.7	(19)	68.3	(16)
Intestate	50.3	(4)	52.9	(10)	58.2	(23)

SOURCE: Essex County Probate Docket and Beverly and Wenham tax lists and reconstitution data.

with an average age of fifty-one years for those who died during the last half of the eighteenth century. Those who lived longest were yeomen and husbandmen, men who escaped the risks of the maritime life. Gentlemen, professionals, and traders died at about the same ages as farmers, although they were less long-lived after 1800. Artisans, as a group, fell between the farmers and the mariners in their mean ages at death. The patterns in Wenham were somewhat comparable, although few mariners or artisans lived there. Farmers lived longest, followed by the gentlemen of Wenham.

The decision to leave a will or not, however, was not simply the result of inadequate estate planning. Among the men who died after 1750 in Beverly, farmers with wills averaged seventy years of age at death; those who died intestate averaged sixty years at their deaths. The same was true in Wenham. Farmers, gentlemen, and traders all died at relatively advanced ages regardless of whether they made a will, suggesting that economic resources were allocated long before fathers died (see Table 6–4). In contrast, mariners in Beverly who died with wills were

TABLE 6–4. *Two-way Analysis of Variance of Mean Age at Death among Male Decedents in Beverly and in Wenham, 1700–1840*

Beverly Occupations	1700–1749		1750–1799		1800–1840	
	Testate	Intestate	Testate	Intestate	Testate	Intestate
Gentlemen, professionals and traders	63 (1)	43 (3)	69 (19)	61 (9)	70 (27)	50 (37)
Shipping and mariners	59 (2)	41 (5)	57 (11)	47 (20)	51 (21)	42 (80)
Artisans	76 (2)	61 (8)	58 (17)	51 (18)	65 (19)	52 (41)
Yeomen and husbandmen	62 (12)	76 (6)	70 (35)	60 (23)	72 (23)	68 (50)
Wenham Occupations						
Gentlemen, professionals, and traders	67 (3)	50 (2)	68 (6)	48 (5)	65 (10)	56 (11)
Yeomen and husbandmen	63 (3)	51 (2)	74 (11)	80 (1)	74 (6)	62 (11)

SOURCE: Essex County Probate Docket and Beverly and Wenham tax lists and reconstitution data.

NOTE: The two-way analysis of variance used in these tables is a factorial design based on two independent variables (occupation and testacy) and one dependent variable (mean age at death). A multiple classification analysis was employed in order to examine the main effects of occupation and testacy on age at death. The tables present the findings of mean ages of death, even though some of the sample sizes were extremely small.

In Beverly, occupation and testacy together explained between 26.8 and 31.8 percent of the proportion of variation in age at death (26.8 percent, 26.8 percent, and 31.8 percent, respectively, for the three time periods). Occupation, however, explained more of the variation in age at death than testacy:

	1700–1749	*1750–1799*	*1800–1840*
beta on occupation	0.51	0.34	0.47
beta on testacy	0.04	0.26	0.27
R^2	0.268	0.268	0.318

Wenham, in contrast to Beverly, revealed declining patterns of variation between occupation and testacy after 1750:

	1700–1749	*1750–1799*	*1800–1840*
beta on occupation	0.50	0.31	0.21
beta on testacy	0.50	0.35	0.29
R^2	0.252	0.306	0.113

The data from Wenham omits "shipping and mariners" and "Artisans" because the numbers were so small as to skew the analysis of variance.

only three years older, on the average, than those who were intestate. More important, mariners were over twenty years younger than farmers when they died.

In Beverly, men who ranked at the top of the economic ladder—gentlemen, professionals, and traders—were similar to the farmers, for there was only an eight-year age difference between those with wills and those without them. In contrast, gentlemen in Wenham during the eighteenth century died at very different ages, with a twenty-year differential between those who had wills and those who died intestate. Most of these gentlemen in Wenham gained their status from wealth, military service, or deference. Gentlemen in Wenham were relatively numerous and did not represent only those who were advanced in age. As a result, many of these men had not contemplated death to the point where they had made out wills. In a sense, gentlemen in Wenham were as surprised by death as were the mariners. With the proportion of gentlemen increasing in Wenham during the last half of the eighteenth century, this concern for one's place in society—and not merely one's wealth—was reflected in their estate planning. They hoped to pass on not only wealth but also social status.[12]

Yeomen and husbandmen, who lacked the claims to higher social status, were more concerned with passing on property. Farmers who died without wills in both Beverly and Wenham were sixty years or older and had probably transferred land and property to their children during their lifetimes.

This evidence on the mean age at death among those who left wills and those who did not suggests a different perspective on one of the central debates among historians of the early New England family: to what degree did parents use economic resources to control their children? John Demos, in studying Plymouth Colony, concluded that there was no clear pattern of parents deploying property to control their children; some did, but others did not. In contrast, Philip Greven's research on colonial Andover, Daniel Scott Smith's analysis of Hingham, and Robert Gross's study of Revolutionary Concord indicate that parents increasingly used land to control their children. The evidence on the social structure of inheritance and intestacy in Beverly and Wenham, as well as the overall pattern of willmaking, suggests that both viewpoints are correct and represent different stages in the development of inheritance as one method for allocating economic resources. During the seventeenth and early eighteenth centuries in Beverly and Wenham, willmaking was common, but declined when the division of common lands freed economic resources. After this division, willmaking rose again in both village and seaport. The group most likely to deploy property to control their children were those of high social status, gentlemen in particular, whereas many farmers, even elderly ones, died intestate.

THE DECLINE OF PARTIBLE INHERITANCE

For historians of colonial New England, one of the major symbols of the openness of the newly settled American colonies was the law of partible inheritance. Unlike England and even the southern colonies in early America, which practiced primogeniture, most of the New England colonies provided that children of parents who died intestate would divide the property equally, saving a double portion for the eldest son. The foremost legal historian of partible inheritance in New England, George Haskins, emphasized the fundamental equality of distribution among children, contrasting the New England practices with those of old England. But Haskins was aware that partible inheritance had an economic rationale: ". . . primogeniture would not only have encouraged the growth of accumulated estates but, more importantly, would have resulted in the impoverishment of younger children in an economy in which the land was the chief form of wealth."[13] Haskins infers that the New England settlers purposefully sought to avoid the accumulation of larger estates through partible inheritance statutes. Charles M. Andrews, in examining the history of inheritance and intestacy in colonial Connecticut, makes much the same point: primogeniture was not only illogical but also would have resulted in an uneven distribution of land.[14] More recently, William Nelson, in describing the legal order of eighteenth-century Massachusetts, speculated that the law of partible inheritance "resulted in a wider distribution of wealth . . . and hence greater economic security among younger children."[15] From the perspective of most legal historians, partible inheritance represented not only a form of property distribution but also a microcosm of the openness of American society.

But for the people of Beverly and Wenham, was the law of partible inheritance adequate, given the demographic and economic constraints of the eighteenth century? Perhaps the law of partibility was unique and innovative during the seventeenth century, but how did this law fare when land was not as abundant as it had been and when parents' concerns for their children were not readily resolved by simply distributing land? Some related evidence suggests that the equal distribution of land through inheritance underwent severe testing during the eighteenth century. In York County, Maine, and Andover, Massachusetts, men who left wills during the eighteenth century gradually moved toward primogeniture—leaving their property in the hands of one son.[16] This evidence suggests that as economic conditions became more constricted, actual inheritance practices—as we have seen in the earlier sections—were not as open as the law of partible inheritance would lead us to believe.

How many intestate men had their estates divided under the rules of partible inheritance? In Beverly, exactly 25 percent required divisions between 1721 and 1800 and by the early nineteenth century, about 15 percent (see Table 6–5). In Wenham, slightly less than one-fourth of the decedents fell within the partible laws, with the proportions declining after 1760. In

TABLE 6–5. *Testate and Intestate Estates in Beverly and in Wenham (males only) 1681–1840*

	Beverly			
	1681–1720	1721–1760	1761–1800	1801–1840
Testate	27%	35%	34%	25%
Intestate				
Division	29%	25%	25%	15%
No Division	44%	39%	41%	60%
Total	(96)	(218)	(282)	(502)
	Wenham			
Testate	42%	50%	51%	49%
Intestate				
Division	21%	23%	17%	18%
No Division	38%	27%	32%	43%
Total	(24)	(48)	(53)	(49)

SOURCE: Essex County Probate Docket.

both Beverly and Wenham, there were no major changes in the proportions of men whose estates were divided among their children; rather, a slow and gradual decline occurred. The more important shift in inheritance practices in Beverly and Wenham was not with the division of intestate estates but with the increase in willmaking. The men of Beverly and Wenham tried to avoid the equality of the partible inheritance system because it was not in their children's interests.

While the concept of partible inheritance remained very much a part of Massachusetts law, probate courts recognized that alternative approaches to settling intestate estates were required. Probate judges appointed "appraisers" or "subscribers" to assist them in partitioning and dividing the estates of those without wills. The appraisers approached their task in two fundamental ways. First, they decided if the estate could be divided "without Prejudice or Spoiling the whole." Probate judges were reluctant to split up estates if the result was worthless parcels of land for the heirs. Clearly, the appraisers recognized that fair market value had to be maintained in dividing the estates of those without wills. For example, the substantial estate of Nathaniel Goodhew of Ipswich, nearby to Beverly and Wenham, was divided into two parcels representing three-sevenths and four-sevenths of the original estate.[17] With Goodhew's estate, the acreage permitted an absolute division of the real property, but only into two new parcels of land. Goodhew died with seventy-nine-and-a-half acres of farm land, twenty-six-and-a-half acres of marsh, a homestead, two dwelling houses, and miscellaneous lots of land. But in another case, the estate of Isaac Ellwell of Gloucester, the probate judge held against a division of property because the appraisers found only four acres of land and three acres of swamp land.[18] Ellwell's land was not subject to a division which maintained fair market value of the land.

Yet Goodhew and Ellwell each left six children who were heirs to his property. Since the land itself could not be divided among all of the children in either case, the probate courts did not attempt to distribute the land in absolute terms. Rather, the appraisers valued the land and the probate court divided it into shares which were distributed according to the requirements of the partible inheritance statute. In cases such as these, when the actual division of the estate did not permit all of the children to inherit land, the eldest son held a "right of redemption" which entitled him to pay his brothers and sisters for their portions of the estate. Isaac Ellwell's eldest son, Eleazar, chose not to exercise his right of redemption, giving it instead to his next oldest brother, Joseph, perhaps because the property was worth only fifty-three pounds. But Nathaniel Goodhew's eldest son did redeem the other five shares held by his two brothers and three sisters. Since Goodhew's estate was a substantial one, valued in 1723 at £1100, he had to pay out over £785. In both cases the intent of the partible inheritance law was fulfilled in only a monetary way, since the remaining brothers and sisters did not enjoy the use and ownership of property. By the early eighteenth century, if not earlier, Essex County probate courts did not break up estates beyond their fair market value. Rather, what prevailed was a conception of property that stressed the use of the land as it existed. To the extent that partible inheritance laws—as administered by the probate courts—actually distributed property, they did so from a conservative perspective, unwilling to permit farms to fall below certain perceived sizes. In neighboring Middlesex County, appraisers also avoided splitting up estates. In Concord, estates that were divided averaged about 160 acres in size, while smaller ones were simply not broken up. Large estates were more vulnerable to partible inheritance laws, which perhaps explains why there was a substantial increase in willmaking during the eighteenth century. In Concord, as in Beverly and Wenham, only a few estates actually came before the probate courts to be divided. Men who owned large estates generally avoided intestacy. In Beverly, for example, only 12 percent of the gentlemen, professionals, and traders had their estates divided by partible inheritance during the last half of the eighteenth century. The estates of mariners and farmers were those which appeared most often before the probate courts as intestate (26 percent of the mariners and 29 percent of the farmers had their estates divided). Artisans did not have their estates divided often, but they also tended not to leave wills. Rather, it was the gentlemen who had more to gain from avoiding probate—and they did.

By the eighteenth century, partible inheritance cannot be seen in the same light as it was during the seventeenth century. Its distributional function—to allocate land to the younger generations—changed to become a holding action against the pressures of division of land and resources. While partible inheritance has been ideologically important to legal historians, by the eighteenth century it served to support the existing distribution of land. It had lost its innovative value. To some extent it aided younger siblings to gain what might be termed an economic stake if their eldest brother could redeem their shares in the estate. But this shift seems more reminiscent of primogeniture, when the eldest son inherited the entire estate. While this was not exactly the case in Massachusetts, the actual *use* of the land did result in constricted patterns of inheritance. Younger brothers and sisters, it seems, had to take their money and move on.

CHAPTER 7

CONCLUSION

THROUGHOUT this exploration of the history of migration in eighteenth-century Beverly and Wenham, our concern has been with the larger patterns of mobility in the American past. All too often "colonial" history appears only as the backdrop against the more dramatic (and more numerous) migration experiences of the nineteenth and twentieth centuries. For example, to Frederick Jackson Turner and his numerous students, the process of migration almost became synonymous with westward movement of the nineteenth century.[1] More recently, the historians of immigration and the new urban historians, for example, Oscar Handlin, Stephan Thernstrom, and Michael Katz, refocused the history of migration around urban life as they examined the people who not only crossed the Atlantic during the nineteenth and twentieth centuries but also of those who migrated from rural America into the modern metropolis.[2] Turner and his students argued that the frontier was the "safety valve" in American culture; whereas Thernstrom suggested that for immigrants, Yankees, and blacks, the city was the "safety valve."

Perhaps it would be best to say that both interpretations are accurate: there was a "double safety valve" of migration. The people of the eastern states moved increasingly to western lands, but with commercial growth and later industrialization, the cities of America filled up with migrants as well. Yet the phenomenon of the "double safety valve" was not unique to modern

America. It first occurred in colonial New England as people sought out new lands in New Hampshire, Maine, and western Massachusetts or moved into seaports like Boston, Salem, and Beverly. The double safety valve of migration to open lands or to commercial centers began in colonial New England. Later, the very same process was repeated as men and their families sought to adapt, through migration, to changing conditions of life.

PATTERNS OF PERSISTENCE: THE MIGRATION TRANSITION

How did the patterns of persistence in Beverly and Wenham compare with those of other colonial New England towns? More generally, how do these patterns compare with those in modern America? The answers to these questions will be limited until there emerge community studies covering the entire span of American history.[3] By employing rates of persistence, standardized at approximately ten-year intervals, we may combine several studies of local communities to construct an overview of the pattern of persistence in America since the settlement of New England in the seventeenth century.[4] This overview provides a framework in which we can appreciate how the mobility experiences of the people of eighteenth-century Beverly and Wenham represented the beginning of a "migration transition."

The American persistence pattern was one of gradual transition from high to low levels of population continuity (see Figure 7–1). Chronologically, three stages of the migration transition appear: in the seventeenth century, very high rates of population persistence; in the eighteenth century, declining rates, with lower rates established firmly in the early nineteenth century; and after that, much lower rates.

In the seventeenth century, the first settlers to New England moved away rather quickly from central areas of population near the seaports. The settlers of Plymouth Colony organized twenty-

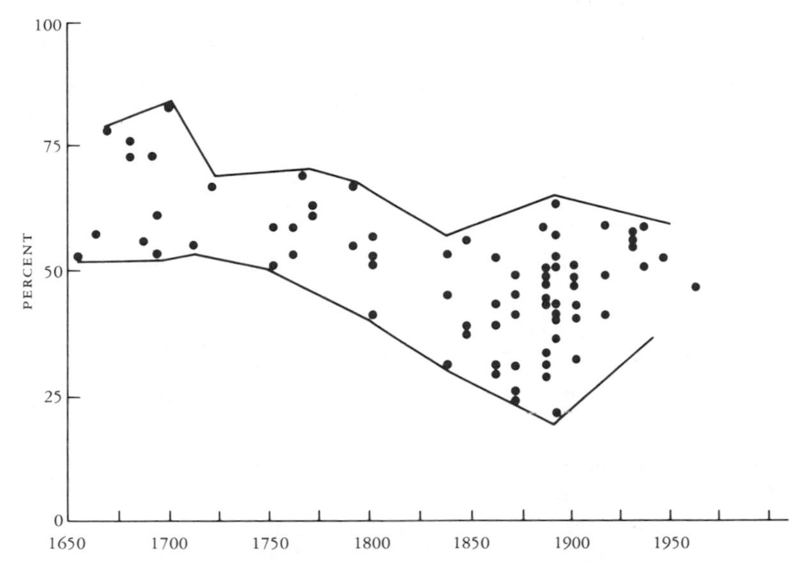

NOTE: Each dot represents a decennial rate of persistence for one or more communities.

FIGURE 7–1. The Migration Transition: Patterns of Persistence in America, 1653–1968

one towns by 1691, spreading out in all possible directions from the center of Plymouth in order to take advantage of unsettled land.[5] Similarly, the settlement of Essex County, Massachusetts, reflected the desire to accumulate landed property. By 1685 the settlers incorporated sixteen towns, and there were numerous hamlets which emerged as towns during the eighteenth century. Middlesex County developed along a similar pattern, with fifteen towns incorporated by 1691. Dispersion of settlement over broad geographical areas in New England almost from the moment of arrival was the common experience. Yet once established in a new town, how long did this first generation of settlers remain?

In two Massachusetts towns, Dedham and Rowley, slightly more than one-half of the first group of taxpayers or landholders continued to live in those towns for a decade or more following initial settlement (see Table 7–1). This similarity between

TABLE 7–1. *Rates of Persistence in Selected Communities in Colonial New England*

Decade	Community[a]	Rate of Persistence	N	Range	Mean
1643–1653	Rowley	59%	(54)		
1648–1660	Dedham	52%	(98)		
1660–1670	Dedham	78%	(91)		
	Hingham	73%	(96)		
1676–1686	Windsor, Conn.	57%	(165)		
1680–1690	Dedham	73%	(113)		
1686–1696	Manchester	61%	(34)		
1687–1695	Boston	53%	(1124)		
1690–1700	Dedham	83%	(125)	52–83%	67%
1723–1733	Dedham	55%	(204)		
1731–1741	Dedham	68%	(99)		
1741–1751	Beverly	50%	(302)		
	Wenham	58%	(113)		
1751–1761	Beverly	58%	(304)		
	Wenham	53%	(105)		
1754–1765	Hingham	69%	(331)		
1761–1771	Beverly	64%	(368)		
	Wenham	59%	(99)		
1780–1790	Boston	56%	(2225)		
1790–1800	Hingham	68%	(347)	50–69%	60%

NOTE: In the persistence rate, the denominator was the number of persons listed in the first time period, and the numerator, the persons who continued to the following time period. All persistence rates in this table have been standardized to fit this method of calculation.

[a] Sources, in order of listing: calculated by the author from *The Early Records of the Town of Rowley, Massachusetts, 1639–1672* (Rowley: privately printed, 1894), v-x; Kenneth A. Lockridge, "The Population of Dedham, Massachusetts, 1636–1736," *Economic History Review,* 19 (1966), 322; Daniel Scott Smith, "Population, Family, and Society in Hingham, Massachusetts, 1635–1880," (unpublished dissertation, University of California, Berkeley, 1973); Linda Auwers Bissell, "From One Generation to Another: Mobility in Seventeenth-Century Windsor, Connecticut," *William and Mary Quarterly,* 31 (1974), 79–110; calculated by the author from *Manchester Town Records, 1636–1736* (Salem: privately printed, 1889), 30–31; 73; James A. Henretta, "Economic Development and Social Structure in Colonial Boston," *William and Mary Quarterly,* 22 (1965), 74–92; tax list and reconstitution data of Wenham, Massachusetts; tax list and reconstitution data of Beverly, Massachusetts; Allan Kulikoff, "The Progress of Inequality in Revolutionary Boston," *William and Mary Quarterly,* 28 (1971), 402.

All towns listed are located in Massachusetts unless otherwise noted.

Dedham and Rowley suggests that there was a natural process of population growth and settlement, from lower to higher rates of persistence. This settling-out process, by which families and individuals chose one town rather than another, was repeated in numerous New England towns.[6]

Overall, the mean persistence rate of selected New England towns during the seventeenth century was 67 percent. Once the first generation had settled in, persistence rates in New England towns during the seventeenth century ranged between 52 and 83 percent, suggesting that some, but not all, of the towns had extremely stable populations. Well into the seventeenth century, some towns, such as Boston and Windsor, Connecticut, maintained persistence rates very similar to those to be found during the first decades of their settlement. As the major port of entry in New England, Boston's population was obviously more mobile than that of a small farming town. Windsor, on the other hand, was located on the edge of the frontier and was a stepping-off point for some migrants. The general trend in New England towns during the seventeenth century was toward permanent settlement. Between 1660 and 1700, more taxpayers chose to remain in their towns of residence than did the first generation of settlers.

By the eighteenth century, persistence rates had declined. This change in persistence rates during the eighteenth century occurred at the high end of the spectrum, with the maximum rates of continuity dropping. At the low end of the spectrum, however, rates never fell below 50 percent. The extremely high rates of persistence, such as those over 80 percent in Dedham, dropped after 1730, with a more narrow range of persistence rates to be found during the eighteenth century. The change from the seventeenth to the eighteenth centuries was gradual, with the mean persistence rate declining by only seven percentage points (60 percent).

For example, Boston's persistence rate was just over 50 percent in 1780–1790. Yet tiny farming populations, such as Wenham's, also exhibited persistence rates at the minimum level of about 50 percent. Rural and urban rates of persistence seemed to be moving in the same direction—implying more mobility in the society as a whole.

Declining persistence rates reflected both the search for open lands and economic opportunity and the changes in population structure. The result was that migration in the eighteenth century limited the size of many New England towns, particularly the older ones in the eastern counties. Without efficient birth control practices, migration was the only means of controlling the growth of the population. The declining persistence pattern, dating at least from the 1730s in Massachusetts, was the beginning of the long-term transition to the lower persistence rates of the nineteenth and twentieth centuries.

Since 1800, both rural and urban rates of persistence in America were sharply lower than those to be found in colonial New England. Among nineteenth-century rural communities, the range of persistence rates varied between 21 and 59 percent, quite a sharp drop from the eighteenth-century experience. Similarly, the average persistence rate of nineteenth-century rural communities was 41 percent, only two-thirds as high as the eighteenth-century average. Of course, frontier farm settlements were characterized by high population turnover if the point of comparison is the New England town of the seventeenth century (see Table 7–2).

Urban communities in nineteenth-century America were more varied in their persistence rates than the colonial cities. Boston's rate of persistence between 1830 and 1850 was about 40 percent, well below what it had been in 1790. But the overall range of rural and urban persistence rates in the nineteenth century was more similar than different. Also, the average persistence rate of urban centers in the nineteenth century was 47 percent, close to the rural average. Similarities in the range of persistence

TABLE 7–2. *Rates of Persistence in Selected Rural and Urban Communities in Nineteenth-Century America*

Decade Rural	Community	Rate of Persistence	Overall Range 21–59%	Overall Mean 41%
1800–1810	Ware, Mass.	56%		
	Northampton, Mass.	52%		
	Pelham, Mass.	43%		
1850–1860	Wapello County, Iowa	30%		
1860–1870	Trempealeau County, Wisconsin	25%		
	Eastern Kansas	26%		
	East Central Kansas	31%		
	Central Kansas	42%		
1870–1880	Trempealeau County	29%		
	Roseburg, Oregon	34%		
	Eastern Kansas	44%		
	East Central Kansas	59%		
1885–1895	Grant County, Wisc.	21%		
	Eastern Kansas	51%		
	East Central Kansas	51%		
	Central Kansas	46%		
Urban			30–64%	47%
1800–1810	Salem, Mass.	52%		
1830–1840	Boston, Mass.	44%		
	Philadelphia, Pa.	30%		
	Waltham, Mass.	54%		
1840–1850	Boston	39%		
	Philadelphia	38%		
	Waltham	56%		
1850–1860	Boston	39%		
	Philadelphia	32%		
	Waltham	44%		
	Northampton, Mass.	53%		
1860–1870	Waltham	45%		
	Poughkeepsie, N.Y.	49%		

TABLE 7–2. (*continued*).

Decade Urban	Community	Rate of Persistence	Overall Range 30–64%	Overall Mean 47%
1870–1880	Waltham	50%		
	Poughkeepsie	50%		
	Atlanta	44%		
	San Antonio, Texas	32%		
	San Francisco	48%		
1880–1890	Boston	64%		
	Waltham	58%		
	Omaha	44%		
	Los Angeles	54%		
	San Francisco	50%		

SOURCE: Stephan Thernstrom, *The Other Bostonians: Poverty and Progress in the American Metropolis 1880–1970* (Cambridge, Massachusetts: Harvard University Press, 1973), 222; 226; Tables 9.1 and 9.2.

rates, not differences, characterize the history of population turnover in the nineteenth century and in the twentieth century, when rural and urban persistence rates remained within the pattern established a century before (see Table 7–3). The volatile turnover of the nineteenth-century frontier towns disappeared as the persistence rates clustered between 40 and 60 percent. This same trend toward stability within a pattern of wide diversity may also be detected in the slightly increased average persistence rate during the twentieth century, which rose to 52 percent. While the twentieth-century pattern continued to reflect the diversity established during the early-nineteenth century, it fell within the same general range.

For Massachusetts, the eighteenth century was a transitional stage for migration. To sharpen the contrast between colonial and modern persistence rates in America, we may employ a "refined" persistence rate. This measure, which accounts for mortality by controlling for persons who died within each decade,

TABLE 7–3. *Rates of Persistence in Selected Communities in Twentieth-Century America*

Decade Rural and Urban	Community	Rate of Persistence	Overall Range 33–59%	Overall Mean 52%
1895–1905	Eastern Kansas	48%		
	East Central Kansas	51%		
	Central Kansas	40%		
	West Central Kansas	47%		
	West Kansas	33%		
1900–1910	Omaha	44%		
1910–1920	Boston	41%		
	Los Angeles	49%		
	Norristown, Pa.	59%		
1925–1935	Eastern Kansas	55%		
	East Central Kansas	56%		
	Central Kansas	56%		
	West Central Kansas	58%		
	West Kansas	51%		
1930–1940	Boston	59%		
	Norristown	50%		
1940–1950	Norristown	53%		
1958–1968	Boston	46%		

SOURCE: Stephan Thernstrom, *The Other Bostonians: Poverty and Progress in the American Metropolis 1880–1970* (Cambridge, Massachusetts: Harvard University Press, 1973), 222, Tables 9.1 and 9.2.

yields relatively higher rates than the "crude" one, for the "refined" rate tells us only what proportion of a *surviving* population persisted. Clearly, mortality changes the complexion of a community's population, but theoretically changes which result from migration carry greater social implications.

The overall pattern of transition from the seventeenth to the twentieth century is confirmed in Table 7–4 in these "refined" rates. There was a slight decrease from the seventeenth to the eighteenth centuries but a more dramatic difference when the

TABLE 7–4. *Crude and Refined Rates of Persistence in Selected Communities,* 1643–1950

Year	Community	Crude Rate	Refined Rate	Difference
1676–1688	Clayworth, England	51%	78%	27%
1643–1653	Rowley, Mass.	59%	71%	12%
1648–1660	Dedham, Mass.	52%	63%	9%
1660–1670		78%	88%	10%
1670–1680		76%	93%	17%
1680–1690		73%	91%	18%
1690–1700		83%	96%	13%
1676–1686	Windsor, Conn.	57%	71%	14%
1741–1751	Beverly, Mass.	50%	66%	16%
1751–1761		58%	67%	9%
1761–1771		68%	72%	4%
1731–1741	Wenham, Mass.	68%	76%	8%
1741–1751		58%	67%	9%
1751–1761		53%	70%	17%
1761–1771		60%	67%	7%
1910–1920	Norristown, Penn.	59%	66%	7%
1930–1940		50%	58%	8%
1940–1950		53%	57%	4%

SOURCES: See notes to Table 7–1, for Rowley, Dedham, Windsor, Beverly and Wenham. For Clayworth, see Peter Laslett and John Harrison, "Clayworth and Cogenhoe," in H. E. Bell and R. L. Ollard, eds., *Historical Essays, 1600–1750, Presented to David Ogg* (London: A. and C. Black, 1964), 157–84. The Norristown rates are from Sidney Goldstein, *Patterns of Mobility 1910–1950: The Norristown Study* (Philadelphia: University of Pennsylvania Press, 1958).

pre-1800 rates are compared with those of the twentieth century. In the seventeenth century, for example, Dedham had "refined" persistence rates of over 90 percent in some decades, truly a stable population. But a century later, Beverly and Wenham had lower persistence rates, ranging from 66 to 76 percent. This downward trend in the "refined" persistence rates continued in Norristown, Pennsylvania, with a rate of about 58 percent in 1930 and 1950. Thus, when mortality is taken into account, the transition in the persistence rate over time remains.

Just as there was a demographic transition from high fertility and mortality rates to lower ones, so too was there a migration transition. During the eighteenth century, at least in New England, population and land pressures caused increased migration. By the nineteenth and twentieth centuries, mobility was even more common. Yet it was during the nineteenth and twentieth centuries that the crude birth rate fell, the technology of birth control advanced, and family limitation reduced the overall size of the population.[7] But still migration increased as people moved from job to job and community to community. If migration were mechanistically tied to fertility, we would have expected increased population stability in our times. Such was the not the case. As it did during the eighteenth century, internal migration in Massachusetts continued to adjust the balance between economic resources and people.

The evidence presented here indicates that population mobility increased in incidence and shifted in its social effects between the mid-eighteenth century and the early nineteenth. Ultimately, each stage in the history of population mobility in America must be explained in fuller terms than this overview permits. Yet this framework accentuates both the rate and chronological changes in mobility. Our assumptions of a stable—almost motionless—New England society before 1800 are only partially true. Population mobility in the New England towns examined here varied from century to century and community to community, suggesting that there was no single, typical mobility rate for the New England town. Yet there were striking differences between colonial and nineteenth- and twentieth-century communities, indicating there may have been more variation in persistence patterns in the 170 years prior to 1800 than in the following ones.

THE DISPERSION OF SETTLEMENTS: THE DOUBLE SAFETY VALVE

As we have seen with the people of Beverly and Wenham, population movement in the eighteenth century was not limited to farmers moving rapidly and in huge numbers to the frontier. Rather, there was a double safety valve of out-migration to unsettled lands in New Hampshire and Maine as well as movement into the commercial seaports. Commercial growth during the late eighteenth century provided an additional outlet for the dynamics of internal population movement. Of course, other economic alternatives were important as the people of eastern Massachusetts adjusted to the problems of land scarcity. Some men sought to improve their farming techniques to increase productivity, others enlisted in the colonial armies to gain freedom from servitude as well as to gain land bounties, and still others turned to the sea as an economic alternative. Yet each of these economic options required either migration (to take advantage of land bounties) or commercial growth (maritime trade required access to port cities while farmers had to rely on expanding marketplaces). While eighteenth-century Massachusetts was still an agricultural, rather than an industrial society, commercial growth during the late eighteenth century began to sweep people into the port towns, thus serving as the second safety valve. Well before the nineteenth century, migrants in colonial Massachusetts sought opportunities in both commercial centers and on the frontier.

With migration within the New England region occurring during the eighteenth century, one would expect new settlements to have been formed within Massachusetts as well. A chronology of settlement formation before 1860 permits us to plot the rise and then the decline in migration as a solution to population growth. By quantifying the number of settlements formed within Massachusetts by geographic region, one can measure the extent of geographic dispersion of the population during the eighteenth century. This was done by dividing Massachusetts into two regions: the east, which includes all of the counties to the east of Worcester County, and the west, encompassing Worcester and all counties to the west. Settlements, in this context, include all towns, districts, and plantations at the dates of their first formation.[8] Districts, unlike towns, could not send a representative to the General Court. By 1702, districts appointed their own clerks, supported their ministers, and enforced the collection of taxes.[9] Plantations had less political autonomy but still were viewed as distinct settlements.

The formation of settlements based on the political unit of the town may reveal more about the politics of town chartering than secular trends in geographic dispersion. For example, the limitation of the powers of the districts to send representatives to the General Court was related to Anglo-American politics. In 1743, the King forbade the incorporation of new towns without his approval. According to the Board of Trade he believed that new town formation produced many "inconveniences and particularly that of increasing the number of Representatives [to the General Court]. . . ." In 1761, the General Court specifically stated that districts held all powers of the town except representation. Clearly, the growth of the population in Massachusetts produced domestic and foreign political tensions. By 1775, the General Court, embued with the spirit of revolution, swiftly incorporated all districts into towns. This act was an attempt to integrate all districts into the political process of revolution; their position in the social order was established.[10]

Most seventeenth-century communities were located in eastern Massachusetts (see Figure 7–2). Only about ten settlements were formed in western Massachusetts before 1700, primarily around the area of Springfield and Northampton, while six times that number were formed along the east coast. By 1740, there was an absolute decline in the number of settlements formed in the east when communities in the western frontier

FIGURE 7–2. Settlement Formation in Massachusetts, 1621–1860

sprang up. During the middle decades of the eighteenth century, 90 percent of all new settlements between 1741 and 1780 were located in the western counties. Since Maine and New Hampshire were not included within this analysis, the proportion of settlements outside the eastern counties was probably higher. While the creation of communities ebbed in the eastern counties, it peaked among the frontier counties of Massachusetts during the mid-eighteenth century.

Population dispersion into the western counties began to decline about 1780. Probably at no other period was the population of Massachusetts as evenly distributed between the eastern and western counties as in 1800.[11] Yet this balance was only temporary; by 1820, patterns of settlement formation in eastern and western Massachusetts converged again. The earlier shift in 1740 represented the first, most immediate response of an agricultural society to the need for more land—geographic mobility.

The second change in regional settlement patterns, which occurred between 1781 and 1820, was related to foreign immigration, rural to urban migration, and the beginnings of industrialization. Instead of becoming relatively depopulated as a result of migration in the mid-eighteenth century, the towns in the eastern counties began to absorb this flow of humanity as an industrializing economy drew men and women from the farms of both New England and Europe into mills and factories. This second pattern of community growth returned the eastern counties to their dominant position in terms of population size because of economic growth, foreign immigration, and rural to urban migration.

Thus a major response to the growth of the population during the early eighteenth century was out-migration. New settlements mushroomed in western Massachusetts as the eastern counties, especially its farming towns, became overpopulated. Yet the surge of new and subdivided communities which had characterized the history of eastern Massachusetts came to a halt by 1740, as people moved to the western counties and to New Hampshire (see Figure 7–3). Even western settlements attained their peak numbers, gradually ending by 1780. Moreover, subdivided settlements declined in number in the western counties by 1780. Town formation and subdivision in the western counties leveled off during the next forty years and declined sharply after 1820 because the supply of western lands had been exhausted.

During the mid-eighteenth century, subdivision of settlements in the east almost came to a standstill as out-migration replaced land redistribution as an alternative economic choice among farmers. Land division had reached its natural limits. Commercial growth in port towns provided another, albeit less dramatic,

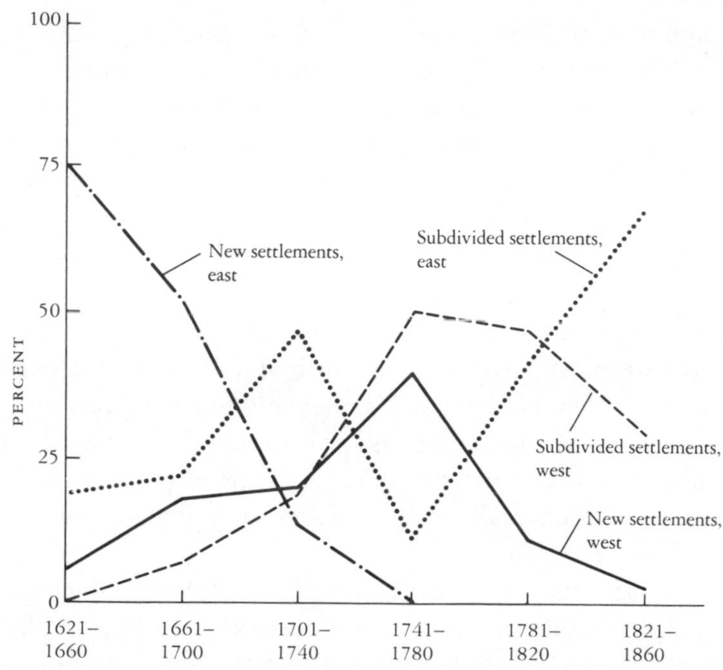

FIGURE 7–3. Settlement Formation in Massachusetts, 1621–1860, by Geographic Region and Type of Settlement

alternative for maturing sons and migrants in eastern Massachusetts. But after about 1780, subdivision of towns in the eastern counties suddenly reoccurred, surpassing the levels of town subdivision of the seventeenth century. Commercialization, and later industrialization, provided another "safety valve" for population growth in some late eighteenth century communities and in many more during the early-nineteenth century. Out-migration was but one, although important, response to population growth. Ultimately, migration and economic development in commercial centers combined to provide outlets for the dynamics of population growth in colonial as well as modern America.

BEVERLY AND WENHAM: TOWARD A NEW STABILITY

This investigation of migration in Beverly and Wenham leads to a new understanding of the people of the eighteenth-century New England towns. Historians have often portrayed the towns of eighteenth-century New England as "declining," whether it was because of religious declension, the loss of communitarian idealism, economic stratification, or the assumption of English customs.[12] The picture from Beverly and Wenham, at least, seems less bleak. The prevalence of migration fostered social stability rather than limited it. Adaptation was the single most common characteristic of the people of the village and seaport. In particular, migration to unsettled land as well as to commercial towns provided crucial economic opportunities in response to population growth. This stabilizing impulse of migration occurred in other areas of life in Beverly and Wenham: marital formation, inheritance and economic mobility. The old rules for maintaining social order—growing up in the town where one was born, gaining access to land easily, and maintaining close contacts with one's immediate family—were not suddenly changed. Rather, the eighteenth century marked the beginning of a long process in America when internal migration successfully reallocated people and economic resources. As a result, it realigned the patterns of social stability.

With a rapidly growing population in Massachusetts during the eighteenth century, one would expect that migration for economic opportunities would have depopulated towns like Beverly and Wenham. This model of depopulation, however, held true for Wenham only, since it was a tiny agricultural town of but seven square miles. In nearby Beverly, the other half of the double safety valve—movement to commercial towns—resulted in an expanding population during the eighteenth century. Still, native sons rather than migrants in both towns achieved the greatest economic success. The prospects of newcomers were better in Beverly than in Wenham, and some migrants did make considerable gains. Beverly and Wenham, like most New England seaports and villages, had to cope with the problem of land scarcity in the eighteenth century. But the model of out-migration, which has dominated the town studies of early New England, overlooks the role of the commercial town as a magnet for migrants.

Migration also affected personal and familial relationships. It has been commonplace to assume that in colonial Massachusetts towns, the pace and tone of daily life was limited to social interactions among persons who lived only within the boundaries of the same town. The town has been portrayed as an organic whole, almost miraculously satisfying the needs of all of its members. Rather, the evidence from Beverly and Wenham indicates the importance of the local region. Marital partners, for example, sought out each other from the towns directly contiguous to Beverly and Wenham but rarely beyond. Nonresident landowners were common and accepted. Laborers moved about from town to town searching for jobs, as long as they avoided the poor law warnings. Economic relationships among local traders were limited to a confined geographical area. These face-to-face interactions of the people of Beverly and Wenham indicate that social, economic, and personal networks were mobile, yet highly localized *among* neighboring towns and not limited by the political boundaries of the town. By the late eighteenth and early nineteenth centuries, though, newcomers became absorbed in the society and family life of the New England town.

Eighteenth-century Beverly and Wenham were divided into three distinct groups: continuous residents, migrants, and transients. Permanent residents of both Beverly and Wenham provided these towns with social and political leadership. If we ever needed to isolate those who exercised control over what Michael Zuckerman has called the "peaceable kingdoms," it would be this group. They held prominent town offices, served in the militia, were members and deacons of the churches, and were fathers who often unsuccessfully sought to find land for their children. Migrants, on the other hand, were less wealthy. But there were some migrants who did quite well, and moved on again and again, searching for better opportunities. Most transients, though, were poor, migrant laborers seeking work. They were constantly on the move and were governed by the Massachusetts poor laws as administered by the town officials and the Essex County courts.

Localism, or the "town born" in William Bentley's words, no longer guaranteed the homogeneity of the New England town. Yet social cohesion did not disappear. To be sure, migration constantly reshuffled the population of Beverly and Wenham. But parents tried to provide for their children through their wills and deeds of gift more carefully than they had before. Even town policies were changed in order to provide more land for maturing children. Rather than describing a "declining" New England town during the eighteenth century, we should look instead at the adjustments and even the continuities that occurred in order to maintain the social order. Indeed, the resiliency of the men and women of Beverly and Wenham is striking. Faced with economic constriction and population growth, many turned to migration and moved to unsettled towns or to a commercial town. For many, migration was an act of continuity, a way to preserve what they had known and wished to carry forth. Hundreds of men and women from Beverly and Wenham drew deeply upon their inner resources and made commitments to begin life anew. Little did they know that their fate would be tied in a symbolic way to those who would later migrate to the frontier or to the nineteenth-century city.

APPENDIX

The Calculation of Population Turnover in Eighteenth-Century Beverly and Wenham

WHEN measuring population turnover in colonial New England, the researcher is often confronted with a variety of methodological problems. Missing records, incomplete recording systems (especially the vital records), and similar names among the inhabitants all are factors which contribute to potential ambiguity in calculating rates of population turnover.[1] In analyzing population turnover, the critical issue is the appearance and disappearance of people as a result of migration and mortality. Historians of early New England have approached these problems in two basic ways. First, some historians, such as Philip J. Greven, Jr., and Daniel Scott Smith, reconstituted families in such a way as to minimize the effects of fragmentary evidence. In his study of Andover, Greven reconstituted the descendants of the initial settlers of the town, eliminating new persons who moved into the town, and creating "generations" based on the families of these first inhabitants.[2] Daniel Scott Smith, in his study of Hingham, reconstructed the residentially stable families of the town in the colonial period, omitting the migrants.[3] Both approaches permit effective control over the quality of the data needed for family reconstitution but do not afford comparable measures of population turnover such as the decennial migration statistic.

A second approach was employed by Kenneth A. Lockridge in his analysis of the population of colonial Dedham. He examined the extent to which inhabitants on the tax lists of the towns appeared, moved, or died. But because of missing information, Lockridge distinguished among those taxpayers known to have been on the tax lists, those who had "since" died or moved on, and others who had "possibly" died or moved.[4] In effect, Lockridge employed what were low and high estimates of population turnover, depending on the inclusion or exclusion of unidentifiable taxpayers. While Lockridge's approach provides a useful decennial measurement of population turnover and persistence, ambiguity remains because of the unknowns.

Since one of the primary goals of this study was to establish decennial rates of population turnover and persistence for Beverly and Wenham, yet identify as many inhabitants as possible, a third approach was adopted. All taxpayers of eighteenth-century Beverly and Wenham became the base population from which family reconstitution for both towns proceeded. This method permitted the identification of migrants, the linkage of continuous residents from tax list to tax list, and the detection of those who died. Yet unknowns still remained. Rather than omitting the unknown taxpayers, or even creating both low and high rates of population turnover, this study examined the bias of the data with and without the presence of the unknown data. This approach uses the available evidence by estimating the influence of the unknowns on both mortality and migrant status.

Perhaps the most difficult problem is mortality. One could consider all the unknowns to have died, which would yield a low estimate of migration. This "mortality assumption" is used commonly by researchers investigating mortality rates, for they assume the absence of an individual from the death records to be evidence of mortality, yielding a maximum mortality rate.[5] While this approach is sound when analyzing a population's mortality rates, it does not necessarily apply to the study of adult migrants. Equally important is the fact that footloose migrants may have entered and left the tax lists of Beverly and Wenham,

TABLE A–1. *High and Low Estimates of Out-migration in Beverly and in Wenham, Massachusetts, 1731–1771*

	Beverly, 1741–1761, collapsed			
Number of Appearances[a]	Low Estimate[b] Number	Low Estimate[b] Percentage	High Estimate[c] Number	High Estimate[c] Percentage
One	(124)	70%	(198)	70%
Two +	(53)	30%	(86)	30%
Total	(177)	100%	(284)	100%

	Wenham, 1731–1761, collapsed			
Number of Appearances[a]	Low Estimate[b] Number	Low Estimate[b] Percentage	High Estimate[c] Number	High Estimate[c] Percentage
One	(57)	71%	(81)	76%
Two +	(23)	29%	(26)	24%
Total	(80)	100%	(107)	100%

[a] Number of appearances represent the total number of times a taxpayer appeared on the tax lists. In Beverly, tax lists between 1741 and 1771, decennially, were used. In Wenham, taxpayers were drawn from the period, 1731–1771, also decennially. If a taxpayer appeared only in 1771, this appearance is omitted.

[b] The low estimate includes only clearly identifiable out-migrants, based on family reconstitution, and excludes unknown or ambiguous cases.

[c] The high estimate includes both clearly identifiable and unknown or ambiguous cases.

appearing only once, leaving little or no evidence of their existence. This "migration assumption" is particularly important since most migrants were young and were more likely to have changed residences than have died. Table A–1 shows the rates of out-migration in Beverly and Wenham to be remarkably comparable when the low estimate (which excludes the unknowns) is compared with the high estimate (with the unknowns). In effect, there is minimal bias introduced into the rates of out-migration when the unknown taxpayers are included.

One test of the accuracy of the low and high estimates of out-migration presented in Table A–1 is to compare the decennial mortality rates for taxpayers in Beverly and Wenham with those from other New England towns. As Table A–2 illustrates, five eastern New England towns, all founded during the seventeenth century, had decennial rates of mortality of taxpayers which fell between 16 and 19 percent. Beverly was toward the high end of

TABLE A–2. *Decennial Death Rates in Selected New England Towns before 1800*

Decade	Town	Adult, Male Death Rates
1643–1653[a]	Rowley, Mass.	16.6%
1660–1700[b]	Dedham, Mass.	15.6%
1676–1686[c]	Windsor, Conn.	19.0%
1731–1771[d]	Wenham, Mass.	15.9%
1741–1771[d]	Beverly, Mass.	18.5%
Range		15.6 to 19.0%

[a] Calculated from *The Early Records of the Town of Rowley, Massachusetts, 1639–1672* (Rowley: privately printed, 1894), v–x.

[b] Decennial data aggregated from Kenneth A. Lockridge, "The Population of Dedham, Massachusetts, 1636–1736," *Economic History Review,* 19 (1966), 322, Figure 3.

[c] Linda Auwers Bissell, "From One Generation to Another: Mobility in Seventeenth-Century Windsor, Connecticut," *William and Mary Quarterly,* 31 (1974), 104, Table VIII.

[d] Data from Wenham and Beverly tax lists and reconstitution forms. Decennial rates were aggregated.

the spectrum while Wenham was at the low end.[6] Although the total number of towns presented here is small, the fact that Beverly and Wenham fit so closely within the range lends support to the use of the high estimate of out-migration.

Bias in the low and high estimates of in-migrants in Beverly and Wenham is more complex. Table A–3 shows that in Wenham, which had very few unidentifiable taxpayers, the high estimate of in-migrants was not much different than the low one. Because in-migrants were more likely than native sons to be repeating migrants, the high estimate is greater for those who appeared only once and lower for those appearing two or more times. In the same way, including the unknowns in the high estimate of out-migrants in Beverly corrects the impression that the population of that town was residentially stable. Since many of the taxpayers of Beverly seem to have had no official existence in the town except for their appearance on a tax list, it is critical that they be included in a calculation of rates of population turnover. To do otherwise would bias the findings toward stability. This study, then, employs the high estimates of migration and persistence for both Beverly and Wenham.

TABLE A–3. *High and Low Estimates of In-migration in Beverly and in Wenham, Massachusetts, 1731–1771*

	Beverly, 1741–1761, collapsed			
Number of	Low Estimate[b]		High Estimate[c]	
Appearances[a]	Number	Percentage	Number	Percentage
One	(56)	51%	(129)	65%
Two +	(54)	49%	(71)	36%
Total	(110)	100%	(200)	101%

	Wenham, 1731–1761, collapsed			
Number of	Low Estimate[b]		High Estimate[c]	
Appearances[a]	Number	Percentage	Number	Percentage
One	(33)	65%	(46)	70%
Two +	(18)	35%	(20)	30%
Total	(51)	100%	(66)	100%

[a] Number of appearances represent the total number of times a taxpayer appeared on one of the tax lists studied. In Beverly, tax lists between 1741–1771, decennially, were used. In Wenham, taxpayers were drawn from the period 1731–1771, also decennially. If a taxpayer appeared only in 1771, this appearance is omitted.

[b] The low estimate includes only clearly identifiable in-migrants, based on family reconstitution, and excludes unknown or ambiguous cases.

[c] The high estimate includes both clearly identifiable and unknown or ambiguous cases.

BIBLIOGRAPHIC NOTE

This Bibliographic Note is intended to identify both general and specialized studies on migration in colonial America for both general readers and scholars. This brief survey is not exhaustive, and the reader should also consult the notes to each chapter.

Population mobility in old England has fascinated the scholar and general reader alike. One of the more general and provocative studies of the patterns of mobility in England is Peter Laslett, *The World We Have Lost: England Before the Industrial Age* (New York: Charles Scribner's Sons, 1965). For a more detailed analysis of the people of a seventeenth-century English village, see Peter Laslett and John Harrison, "Clayworth and Cogenhoe," in H. E. Bell and R. L. Ollard, eds., *Historical Essays, 1600–1750, Presented to David Ogg* (London: A. and C. Black, 1964), 157–84. For a stimulating essay on the characteristics of migrants who emigrated to the new world, see E. E. Rich, "The Population of Elizabethan England," *Economic History Review,* 2 (1950), 247–65. Two essays review the literature on population mobility in preindustrial England: E. J. Buckatzch, "The Constancy of the Local Populations and Migration in England before 1800," *Population Studies,* 5 (1951–1952), 62–69; and W. R. Prest, "Stability and Change in Old and New England: Clayworth and Dedham," *Journal of Interdisciplinary History,* 6 (1976), 359–74.

The natural starting point for the study of migration in early

New England is with the initial immigrants during the seventeenth century. While one should still consult works such as Marcus Lee Hansen, *The Atlantic Migration, 1607–1860* (Cambridge, Mass.: Harvard University Press, 1940), recent articles have delved more deeply into the social characteristics of the Puritan immigrants. See T. H. Breen and Stephen Foster, "Moving to the New World: The Character of Early Massachusetts Immigration," *William and Mary Quarterly,* 30 (1973), 189–222; and Mildred Campbell, "Social Origins of Some Early Americans," in James Morton Smith, ed., *Seventeenth-Century America: Essays in Colonial History* (Chapel Hill: The University of North Carolina Press, 1959), 63–89. For a reevaluation of Campbell's work, one should look at David W. Galenson, 'Middling People' or 'Common Sort'? The Social Origins of Some Early Americans Reexamined," *William and Mary Quarterly,* 35 (1978), 499–540, which includes a reply by Mildred Campbell. The impact of the new world on the Puritan settlers has long been an important topic, as seen in Sumner Chilton Powell, *Puritan Village: The Formation of a New England Town* (Middletown: Wesleyan University Press, 1963), where group migration and town divisions are examined. The early settlers were quite mobile initially, as John Demos demonstrated in his "Notes on Life in Plymouth Colony," *William and Mary Quarterly,* 22 (1965), 264–86, and more generally in his book, *A Little Commonwealth: Family Life in Plymouth Colony* (New York: Oxford University Press, 1970). Two fascinating and yet quite different case studies of mobility in seventeenth-century New England are: Linda Auwers Bissell, "From One Generation to Another: Mobility in Seventeenth-Century Windsor, Connecticut," *William and Mary Quarterly,* 31 (1974), 79–110; and Ralph J. Crandall, "New England's Second Great Migration: The First Three Generations of Settlement, 1630–1700," *New England Historical and Genealogical Register,* 129 (1975), 347–60.

As the population of Massachusetts (and New England) expanded, land became more scarce. A series of studies have addressed this important question, most notably Philip J. Greven, Jr., *Four Generations: Population, Land, and Family in Colonial Andover, Massachusetts* (Ithaca: Cornell University Press, 1970). The relationship between social development and the American Revolution has been detailed by Robert A. Gross, *The Minutemen and Their World* (New York: Hill and Wang, 1976). Perhaps the most sophisticated explanation of the process of population growth in early New England may be found in Daniel Scott Smith, "The Demographic History of Colonial New England," *Journal of Economic History,* 32 (1972), 165–83. A more general study of the changing nature of the New England town, and its "stability," is Kenneth A. Lockridge, *A New England Town: The First Hundred Years* (New York: W. W. Norton, 1970), which is a history of Dedham. Behind the interpretive sweep of Lockridge's study are several articles vital to the student of migration and society: see "The Population of Dedham, Massachusetts, 1636–1736," *Economic History Review,* 19 (1966), 318–44; "Land, Population, and the Evolution of New England Society 1630–1790," *Past and Present,* 39 (1968), 62–80; and "Social Change and the Meaning of the American Revolution," *Journal of Social History,* 6 (1973), 403–39. A more recent synthesis of the literature on preindustrial America is James A. Henretta, "Families and Farms: *Mentalité* in Pre-Industrial America," *William and Mary Quarterly,* 35 (1978), 3–32.

The history of the migrant poor in early New England may be found in Douglas Lamar Jones, "The Strolling Poor: Transiency in Eighteenth-Century Massachusetts," *Journal of Social History,* 8 (1975), 28–54; and ibid., "Poverty and Vagabondage: The Process of Survival in Eighteenth-Century Massachusetts," *New England Historical and Genealogical Register,* 133 (1979), 243–54. For the impact of migration on eighteenth-century Boston, see Allan Kulikoff, "The Progress of Inequality in Revolutionary Boston," *William and Mary Quarterly,* 28 (1971), 375–412.

Marital migration remains a fascinating but still under-studied area of early New England history. The most accessible discussions of the topic are Greven, *Four Generations;* and Susan L. Norton, "Marital Migration in Essex County, Massachusetts, in the Colonial and Federal Periods," *Journal of Marriage and the Family,* 35 (1973), 406–18.

These books and articles, of course, rely on the rich primary sources for early New England. The materials used in the present study serve as examples of the range of evidence to be found for the history of migration and community life in Massachusetts. Of central importance were the provincial tax lists of Beverly and Wenham, which may be found on microfilm in the Tax and Valuation Lists of Massachusetts Before 1776, Lamont Library, Harvard University, Cambridge, Massachusetts. An invaluable guide to the lists is Ruth Crandall, *Tax and Valuation Lists of Massachusetts Towns Before 1776: Finding List for the Microfilm Edition* (Cambridge, Mass.: Harvard University Press, 1971). Manuscript tax lists are also available in the Town Hall of Wenham; after 1776, for example, see Town Records of Wenham, Massachusetts, Vol. 2, 1783–1803, in the Town Clerk's Office. For Beverly, the Tax Lists of Beverly, 1790–1797, are in the Assessor's Office, City Hall, Beverly, Massachusetts. For the reconstitution of the taxpayers and their families, vital records, genealogies, and private family papers were crucial. These materials have been collected by two major research libraries in the New England area, the New England Historic Genealogical Society in Boston, and the Essex Institute in Salem. Both are central to the study of the people of eighteenth-century Essex County.

In addition to the tax lists and the genealogies, the court houses of New England contain a wealth of material on migration that is only now being tapped. Of special importance are the Essex County Court of General Sessions of the Peace, which kept detailed lists of the migrant poor. These records are now located in the Essex Institute. Also of value for this study were the probate records of Essex County, particularly the Probate Docket, a sixteen-volume listing of those people who died with and without wills before 1840. For suggested approaches to the use of legal records in early American history, see Michael Stephen Hindus and Douglas Lamar Jones, "Quantitative Methods or *Quantum Meruit?* Tactics for Early American Legal History," *Historical Methods,* 13 (1980), 63–74. The best and most comprehensive guide to the court records of Massachusetts is Michael Stephen Hindus, *The Records of the Massachusetts Superior Court and its Predecessors: An Inventory and Guide* (Boston: Commonwealth of Massachusetts, 1977).

In order to glean the everyday experiences of migrants from the early New England records, one must use a variety of sources. The town records for Wenham are printed and remarkably complete. Of special use in this study were *Wenham Town Records, 1707–1731* (Topsfield: The Perkins Press, 1938); and *Wenham Town Records, 1730–1775* (Salem: Newcomb and Gauss, 1940). Account books also provide unusual glimpses into both economic and social relationships in the village and seaport towns of the eighteenth century. Such materials may be found in the Beverly Historical Society, the Wenham Historical Association and Museum, Inc., and the Essex Institute. Finally, the Massachusetts Archives remain a primary source for the public documents of early Massachusetts.

NOTES

PREFACE

1. The literature on migration in America is extensive, but a basic beginning point still remains Frederick Jackson Turner, *The Significance of the Frontier in American History* (New York: Henry Holt and Co., 1920). Among his numerous disciples, Ray Allen Billington has been one of the most articulate and thoughtful students of the American West; for example, see his *The Far Western Frontier* (New York: Harper, 1956). In addition to explaining the settlement of the West, migration has been used to explain the development of the American national character—perhaps too heavy a burden—but the studies are provocative; see Rowland Berthoff, "The American Social Order: A Conservative Hypothesis," *American Historical Review,* 65 (1960), 495–514; and George W. Pierson, *The Moving American* (New York: Alfred A. Knopf, 1973). More recently, historians of social mobility have analyzed migration in the nineteenth-century city; see Stephan Thernstrom, *Poverty and Progress: Social Mobility in a Nineteenth Century City* (Cambridge, Mass.: Harvard University Press, 1964); and ibid., *The Other Bostonians: Poverty and Progress in the American Metropolis, 1880–1970* (Cambridge, Mass.: Harvard University Press, 1973). A substantial theoretical literature devoted to migration also exists, but it, too, has little application to early America. See E. G. Ravenstein, "The Laws of Migration," *Journal of the Royal Statistical Society,* 48 (June 1885), 167–235; and 52 (June 1889), 241–305; Samuel A. Stouffer, "Intervening Opportunities: A Theory Relating Mobility and Distance," *American Sociological Review,* 5 (1940), 845–67; ibid., "Intervening Opportunities and Competing Migrants," *Journal of Regional Science,* 2 (1960), 1–26. The most concise theoretical exposition of the implications of the volume of migration is Everett S. Lee, "A Theory of Migration," *Demography,* 3

(1966), 45–57. For a more general interpretation of migration, see Wilbur Zelinsky, "The Hypothesis of the Mobility Transition," *The Geographical Review,* 61 (1971), 219–49.

2. This position is presented in several books and articles, most notably, Kenneth A. Lockridge, *A New England Town: The First Hundred Years* (New York: W. W. Norton, 1970); ibid., "Land, Population, and the Evolution of New England Society 1630–1790," *Past and Present,* 39 (1968), 62–80; Philip J. Greven, Jr., *Four Generations: Population, Land, and Family in Colonial Andover, Massachusetts* (Ithaca: Cornell University Press, 1970); Robert A. Gross, *The Minutemen and Their World* (New York: Hill and Wang, 1976); Charles S. Grant, *Democracy in the Connecticutt Frontier Town of Kent* (New York: Columbia University Press, 1961); and Richard L. Bushman, *From Puritan to Yankee: Character and the Social Order in Connecticut, 1690–1765* (Cambridge, Mass.: Harvard University Press, 1967). For this same position applied to preindustrial Boston, see Gary B. Nash, *The Urban Crucible: Social Change, Political Consciousness, and the Origins of the American Revolution* (Cambridge, Mass.: Harvard University Press, 1979); and Allan Kulikoff, "The Progress of Inequality in Revolutionary Boston," *William and Mary Quarterly,* 28 (1971), 375–412.

3. Modification of the prevailing social interpretation of early New England society has occurred slowly, often focusing on specific issues such as the degree of wealth inequality; see Gloria L. Main, "Inequality in Early America: The Evidence from Probate Records in Massachusetts and Maryland," *Journal of Interdisciplinary History,* 7 (1977), 559–81. In addition, colonial historians now seem to be more concerned with the attitudes of early Americans and not simply with the structure of their society; see James A. Henretta, "Families and Farms: *Mentalité* in Pre-Industrial America," *William and Mary Quarterly,* 35 (1978), 3–32. A very recent contribution to eighteenth-century town studies is Christopher M. Jedrey, *The World of John Cleaveland: Family and Community in Eighteenth-Century New England* (New York: W. W. Norton, 1979).

4. Douglas Lamar Jones, "The Strolling Poor: Transiency in Eighteenth-Century Massachusetts," *Journal of Social History,* 8 (1975), 28–54; and ibid., "Poverty and Vagabondage: The Process of Survival in Eighteenth-Century Massachusetts," *The New England Historical and Genealogical Register,* 133 (1979), 243–54.

5. The most useful approaches to the history of migration in early

New England towns are found in Greven, *Four Generations;* Kenneth A. Lockridge, "The Population of Dedham, Massachusetts, 1636–1736," *Economic History Review,* 19 (1966), 318–44; and John Demos, "Notes on Life in Plymouth Colony," *William and Mary Quarterly,* 22 (1965), 264–86. Population mobility in preindustrial England has been of special importance to colonial American historians, both for comparative purposes and for methodological direction. For examples, see Peter Laslett and John Harrison, "Clayworth and Cogenhoe," in H. E. Bell and R. L. Ollard, eds., *Historical Essays, 1600–1750, Presented to David Ogg* (London: A. and C. Black, 1964), 157–84; R. S. Schofield, "Age-Specific Mobility in an Eighteenth-Century Rural English Parish," *Annales de Démographie Historique,* (1970), 261–74; E. J. Buckatzch, "The Constancy of Local Populations and Migration in England before 1800," *Population Studies,* 5 (1951–1952), 62–69; and E. E. Rich, "The Population of Elizabethan England," *Economic History Review,* 2 (1950), 247–65. For comparative rates of population mobility in preindustrial, western society, see Peter Laslett, "Le Brassage de la Population en France et en Angleterre aux XVII et XVIII Siècles," *Annales de Démographie Historique,* (1968), 99–109; and, more recently, W. R. Prest, "Stability and Change in Old and New England: Clayworth and Dedham," *Journal of Interdisciplinary History,* 6 (1976), 359–74.

6. For my own purposes, the English historical demographers provided the most useful general guides to the methods of family reconstitution, while the specific town studies of early New England offered the practical application of these methods within the New England sources. See E. A. Wrigley, ed., *An Introduction to English Historical Demography: From the Sixteenth to the Nineteenth Century* (New York: Basic Books, 1966); T. H. Hollingsworth, *Historical Demography* (London: Hodder and Stoughton, 1969); ibid., "The Importance of the Quality of Data in Historical Demography," *Daedalus,* 97 (1968), 415–32; and D. V. Glass and D. E. C. Eversley, eds., *Population in History: Essays in Historical Demography* (London: E. Arnold, 1965). I want also to express thanks to Daniel Scott Smith, who provided invaluable assistance as I schooled myself in the methods of historical demography.

7. This reconstitution of the people of Beverly and Wenham was carried out primarily at the New England Historic Genealogical Society, Boston, Massachusetts. I used published and unpublished genealogies and private papers to reconstitute as many individuals as pos-

sible. Because of the large volume of material examined, individual citations to genealogies are not included. I have described the holdings of the society in some detail; see Douglas Jones, "Research Sources for Family History," *The Family in Historical Perspective: An International Newsletter* (1973). For convenience, the reconstituted taxpayers will be cited as "Beverly and Wenham taxpayers and reconstitution data."

8. For Andover, see Greven, *Four Generations;* for Dedham, see Lockridge, *A New England Town;* and for Sudbury, see Sumner Chilton Powell, *Puritan Village: The Formation of a New England Town* (Middletown: Wesleyan University Press, 1963).

9. Edward M. Cook, Jr., *The Fathers of the Towns: Leadership and Community Structure in Eighteenth-Century New England* (Baltimore: Johns Hopkins University Press, 1977); and Van Beck Hall, *Politics Without Parties: Massachusetts, 1780–1791* (Pittsburgh: University of Pittsburgh Press, 1972).

1. ECONOMY AND SOCIETY

1. *Wenham Town Records, 1730–1775* (Salem: Newcomb and Gauss, 1940), 216–17.

2. Petition of the Selectmen of Beverly, September, 1765, Box 1766–1770, Essex County Court of General Sessions of the Peace, Salem, Massachusetts. The records of the Sessions courts, once housed in the Clerk's Office of the Salem Courthouse, are now located in the Essex Institute, Salem, Mass.

3. This distinction between commercial and farming towns has appeared in several other studies of early New England towns. For a more general discussion of the functions of seaports, see Jacob M. Price, "Economic Function and the Growth of American Port Towns in the Eighteenth Century," *Perspectives in American History,* 8 (1974), 121–86. For Boston, see Allan Kulikoff, "The Progress of Inequality in Revolutionary Boston," *William and Mary Quarterly,* 28 (1971), 375–412. The conflicts between farming and seaport towns may also be seen in Paul Boyer and Stephen Nissenbaum, *Salem Possessed: The Social Origins of Witchcraft* (Cambridge, Mass.: Harvard University Press, 1975).

4. Petition of Joshua Herrick and Others, July, 1754, Box 1752–1756, Essex County Court of General Sessions of the Peace, Salem, Mass.

5. The land pressure model was developed most synthetically by

Kenneth A. Lockridge, "Land, Population and the Evolution of New England Society 1630–1790," *Past and Present,* 39 (1968), 62–80. Lockridge amended his model, primarily to account for commercialization, in his "Afterthought, 1970," in Stanley N. Katz, ed., *Colonial America: Essays in Politics and Social Development* (Boston: Little, Brown and Co., 1971), 485–91. Lockridge extended these same ideas into the Revolutionary era in his essay "Social Change and the Meaning of the American Revolution," *Journal of Social History,* 6 (1973), 405–15. Several case studies, all of inland, farming towns, support the general argument that population was pressing on the supply of land: Philip J. Greven, Jr., *Four Generations: Population, Land, and Family in Colonial Andover, Massachusetts* (Ithaca: Cornell University Press, 1970), Robert A. Gross, *The Minutemen and Their World* (New York: Hill and Wang, 1976); and Charles S. Grant, *Democracy in the Connecticut Frontier Town of Kent* (New York: Columbia University Press, 1961). Commercial growth and movement into the seaports of the eighteenth century remains one of the neglected areas of study in early New England history. This study represents one remedy in our historiography, although the issue has not gone unnoticed; see Gary B. Nash, "Urban Wealth and Poverty in Pre-Revolutionary America," *Journal of Interdisciplinary History,* 6 (1976), 545–84, especially 575–76.

6. Price, "Economic Function and the Growth of American Port Towns," 145–46.

7. Two recent studies of early New England towns present typologies of the towns based on socioeconomic data. In *The Fathers of the Towns* (Baltimore: Johns Hopkins University Press, 1976), Edward M. Cook, Jr., sampled 100 towns from throughout New England, deriving a five-part typology: major cities, major county towns, suburbs attached to the cities or county towns, self-contained farm villages, and frontier towns. While Cook's study focuses more specifically on the nature of political leadership and community life, he has provided valuable information for towns in Essex County that correspond to the findings of this study. He constructed a commercial index for eighteenth-century towns, which revealed that Salem, Newburyport, and Marblehead had the highest per capita level of commercial development of any other town in the county. The small seaports, according to my own categories, revealed slightly higher levels of commercialization than most of the farming towns. A second study which corroborates both my own findings and those of Cook is Van Beck Hall,

Politics Without Parties: Massachusetts, 1780–1791 (Pittsburgh: University of Pittsburgh Press, 1972). Hall's typology focuses on the year 1784 but yields somewhat similar results to Cook. Hall created a "commercial-cosmopolitan" index to compare the degree of economic and social development in all Massachusetts towns. Of the twenty-two Essex County towns in 1784, one-half were in the highest-ranked category of "commercial-cosmopolitanism." Compared with other Massachusetts counties, Essex, again, was far more commercialized. See Hall, *Politics Without Parties,* 5–6; 11–12; 13–19. For more specific data on Essex County, see Van Beck Hall, "Appendices to *Politics Without Parties: Massachusetts, 1780–1791,*" filed at Hillman Library, University of Pittsburgh, 1972, Appendix 3, A–36–A–37; A–43–A–45. Both Cook and Hall conclude that commercial growth occurred regionally within New England and that the extremes of commercialization focused on large cities, with commercial activities spreading out from those commercial centers.

8. For a general description of the New England farm during the late eighteenth century, see Max George Schumacher, *The Northern Farmer and his Markets during the Late Colonial Period* (New York: Arno Press, 1975); for Salem, see Richard J. Morris, "Wealth Distribution in Salem, Massachusetts: The Impact of the Revolution and Independence," *Essex Institute Historical Collections,* 114 (1978), 87–102.

9. Schumacher, *The Northern Farmer,* 25.

10. "Valuation of the Several Counties in the Prov of Mass Bay, 1751," Miscellaneous Bound, 1749–1755, Massachusetts Historical Society, Boston, Mass. The following discussion of land use patterns in Essex County is drawn from the valuation of 1751. I am indebted to David Grayson Allan for calling this source to my attention.

11. The poll tax accounted for the following components of the total taxes paid in Beverly and Wenham:

Poll Tax as a Percentage of Total Tax

Town	*1731*	*1741*	*1751*	*1761*	*1771*	*1790*
Beverly	—	52%	47%	40%	38%	29%
Wenham	55%	48%	32%	33%	38%	25%

12. Because the poll tax was levied on all taxable males, the following analysis excludes the poll tax for purposes of the distribution of wealth. My emphasis in this discussion will be on comparing the proportions of taxes paid by different segments of the populations of each

town. When relying on tax lists, rather than valuation lists, the problem of underassessment as well as regressive taxation may occur. With valuation lists, the actual property owned can be analyzed, rather than the tax assessor's estimate of its worth. Since valuation lists were not available for Beverly and Wenham, the provincial assessment lists were used. To test for underassessment and regressive taxation, I compared the distribution of wealth of the 1771 tax list of Wenham with the 1771 valuation list. (No such valuation list exists for 1771 for Beverly.) The results, presented below, reveal only very slight differences in the distribution of wealth and none serious enough to warrant reconsideration of the sources. In fact, the valuations and the assessed taxes were remarkably similar:

The Distribution of Wealth in Wenham, 1771

Percentage of the Population	*Tax List*	*Valuation List*
0–10	0	0
11–20	0	0
21–30	1.7%	1.7%
31–40	4.2%	2.5%
41–50	3.8%	5.1%
51–60	5.2%	5.1%
61–70	6.5%	8.0%
71–80	9.7%	11.7%
81–90	16.3%	16.0%
91–100	53.6%	49.3%

The 1771 tax list for Wenham is taken from Tax and Valuation Lists of Massachusetts Towns Before 1776, microfilm copy, reel 11, Lamont Library, Harvard University, Cambridge, Mass. The valuation for Wenham may now be conveniently examined in Bettye Hobbs Pruitt, ed., *The Massachusetts Tax Valuation List for 1771* (Boston: G. K. Hall and Co., 1978), 160–64. My own calculations, however, were based on the lists in the *Massachusetts Archives,* vols. 132–34.

13. Comparisons among those persons who were not assessed taxes for real and personal property in Beverly and Wenham were as follows:

Proportions Assessed Zero Taxes

Type of tax	*1741*	*1751*	*1761*	*1771*
Real property				
Beverly	18%	28%	22%	19%
Wenham	29%	22%	20%	26%
Personal property				
Beverly	22%	15%	20%	27%
Wenham	17%	16%	13%	24%

14. The relationship between the wealth rankings of fathers and sons was derived from the following table, in which all tax lists, 1731 through 1771, were grouped together for purposes of enlarging the sample of fathers and sons.

Wealth Rank of Fathers and Sons

Real property	*Beverly*		*Wenham*	
Rank	*Fathers*	*Sons*	*Fathers*	*Sons*
Top 20%	44%	9%	40%	18%
Mid 40%	31%	30%	60%	25%
Low 40%	25%	61%	—	57%
N	(16)	(89)	(10)	(28)

Chi square significant for each town below the 0.05 level.

15. For the occupational sectors of these cities, see Price, "Economic Function and the Growth of the American Port Towns"; for a broader perspective on the economic and political development of these seaports, see Gary B. Nash, *The Urban Crucible* (Cambridge, Mass.: Harvard University Press, 1979).

16. The evidence in the following pages is drawn from the Essex County Probate Docket, Essex County Court House, Salem, Mass. The probate records include men and women who died in Beverly and Wenham between 1638 and 1840, whether they left a will or died intestate (without a will). In both towns, decedents were primarily men, comprising between 79 and 96 percent of the total. The proportions of women who died with property increased, so that by 1801, one-fifth of the decedents were women. Almost all of these women were described as single, spinsters or widows.

Since age and mortality are closely related, it is important to understand the age structure of the decedents. The ages at death for the decedents were not recorded in the probate records, but linkage with vital records and reconstitution data yielded ages for about one-half of the decedents (50.7 percent in Beverly and 52.2 percent in Wenham). The distribution of ages at death of the decedents was similar in both towns. The highest proportion of decedents was sixty years or older and the smallest proportion was under forty years of age. In Beverly, 48 percent of the men died over the age of sixty, whereas in Wenham, 60 percent died at over sixty years. This same distribution of the ages of death for the women was true as well. See Chapters two and six for additional analysis of the probate data.

17. These conclusions are based on the comparison of the Schutz coefficient of inequality among various New England towns. The Schutz coefficient measures wealth inequality on a scale from 0 to 1, with 0 equal to perfect equality and 1 equal to perfect inequality; see Robert R. Schutz, "On the Measurement of Income Inequality," *The American Economic Review,* 45 (1951), 107–22. Beverly and Wenham compare with other towns as follows:

Farming Towns			Seaport Towns		
Date	*Community*	*Schutz*	*Date*	*Community*	*Schutz*
1702	Windsor, Conn.	.45	*1687*	Boston	.49
1741	Wenham		*1741*	Beverly	
	real	.42		real	.46
	personal	.41		personal	.47
1771	Wenham		*1771*	Beverly	
	real	.41		real	.37
	personal	.40		personal	.76
1790	Wenham		*1790*	Beverly	
	real	.45		real	.53
	personal	.49		personal	.69
				Boston	.63

This evidence is from the Beverly and Wenham tax lists, 1741, 1771, and 1790; Linda Auwers Bissell, "From One Generation to Another: Mobility in Seventeenth-Century Windsor, Connecticut," *William and Mary Quarterly,* 31 (1974), 79–103; James A. Henretta, "Economic Development and Social Structure in Colonial Boston," *William and Mary Quarterly,* 22 (1965), 80, 82; and Allan Kulikoff, "The Progress of Inequality in Revolutionary Boston," *William and Mary Quarterly,* 28 (1971), 381, Table II. B.

2. SOURCES OF POPULATION GROWTH

1. William Bentley, *The Diary of William Bentley* (Gloucester, Mass.: Peter Smith, 1962), II, 188.

2. I am relying here on the interpretation presented by Daniel Scott Smith, "The Demographic History of Colonial New England," *Journal of Economic History,* 32 (1972), 165–83; also, see J. Potter, "The Growth of Population in America, 1700–1860," in D. V. Glass and D. E. C. Eversley, eds. *Population in History: Essays in Historical Demography* (London: E. Arnold, 1965), 631–88. One of the central points of Smith's article is to emphasize the importance of low age in

marriage—not mortality—in explaining high fertility rates in colonial New England.

3. In Maine, the population expanded 57 percent from 1770–1780; in New Hampshire, the decennial growth rates after 1750 were: 42 percent between 1750–1760; 37 percent from 1760–1770; and 41 percent from 1770–1780; in Vermont, the growth rate was an incredible 376 percent between 1770–1780. Calculated from U.S. Bureau of the Census, *Historical Statistics of the United States, Colonial Times to 1957* (Washington, D.C.: Government Printing Office, 1960), Series Z 1–19.

The limitations of migration as a means of actually controlling family and population sizes have been discussed by Nathan Keyfitz, "Migration as a Means of Population Control," *Population Studies,* 25 (1971), 63–72; also see Harley L. Browning, "Migrant Selectivity and the Growth of Large Cities in Developing Societies," in National Academy of Sciences, comp., *Rapid Population Growth: Consequences and Policy Implications* (Baltimore: Johns Hopkins University Press, 1971), II, 273–314, esp. 281–84.

4. For example, see Marcus Lee Hansen, *The Atlantic Migration, 1607–1860* (Cambridge, Mass.: Harvard University Press, 1940); and Clifford K. Shipton, "Immigration to New England, 1680–1740," *The Journal of Political Economy,* 44 (1936), 225–39. Professor P. M. G. Harris relies on these studies to date a cyclical trend in foreign immigration before the Revolution; see his "The Social Origins of American Leaders: The Demographic Foundations," *Perspectives in American History,* 3 (1969), 230–34. For a more cautious estimate of levels of immigration, see Potter, "The Growth of Population in America," 644–46.

5. An analysis of the surnames of the heads of households in 1790 suggests that population growth in Massachusetts was not greatly influenced by non-English immigrants. In 1790, 95 percent of the heads of households in Massachusetts were of English origins. New York and Pennsylvania had the most non-English heads of households; see U.S. Bureau of the Census, *A Century of Population Growth* (Washington, D.C., 1909), 116, Table 45.

6. Calculated from Jack and Marion Kaminkow, *A List of Emigrants from England to America 1718–1759* (Baltimore: Magna Charta [sic] Book Co., 1964), 257; and Michael Ghirelli, *A List of Emigrants from*

England to America 1682–92 (Baltimore: Magna Carta Book Co., 1968), xii:

Destinations	Immigrants to America 1682–92	1718–59
New England Colonies	1%	1%
Middle and Southern Colonies	44%	50%
Caribbean Islands	48%	47%
Other	7%	2%
N	(960)	(3080)

7. *Massachusetts Archives,* v. 116, 458–59, 461; 462–64.

8. The net or residual method of analysis is discussed in Sidney Goldstein, *Patterns of Mobility: The Norristown Study* (Philadelphia: University of Pennsylvania Press, 1958), 5–6. Also, see Stephan Thernstrom, *The Other Bostonians: Poverty and Progress in the American Metropolis, 1880–1970* (Cambridge, Mass.: Harvard University Press, 1973), 9–28.

9. In Beverly, the proportion of children under sixteen years was 47 percent in 1765; in Wenham, it was 46 percent. A more precise study of fertility levels by occupational class may reveal differences between the commercial families as compared with the farmers. Proportions of children calculated from Joseph B. Felt, "Statistics of the Population in Massachusetts," *Collections of the American Statistical Association,* I, Part II (Boston, 1845), 149.

10. The net method does not convey the volume of population turnover. Stephan Thernstrom and Peter R. Knights have suggested that total population turnover in nineteenth-century cities was quite high. Similarly high proportions of population turnover in eighteenth-century towns seems improbable, although Beverly undoubtedly encountered more new persons than a farming town such as Wenham. For the nineteenth-century estimates and revisions of their estimates, see Thernstrom, *The Other Bostonians,* 15–28; and Stephan Thernstrom and Peter R. Knights, "Men in Motion: Some Data and Speculations about Urban Population Mobility in Nineteenth-Century America," *Journal of Interdisciplinary History,* 1 (1970), 7–35.

11. The youthfulness of migrants in modern America is well-documented; see Henry S. Shryock, Jr., *Population Mobility Within the United States* (Chicago: University of Chicago Press, 1964), 346–58; Goldstein, *Patterns of Mobility,* 203–06. The average age of long-

term residents in 1761 in Beverly was forty-eight years; in Wenham, it was fifty-one years.

12. This differential has been identified by Maris A. Vinovskis, "Mortality Rates and Trends in Massachusetts before 1860," *The Journal of Economic History,* 32 (1972), 184–213.

13. My purpose here is not to reconstruct the exact parameters of life expectancy in Beverly and Wenham. Rather, I am using mean age at death as a convenient indicator that can be analyzed with other variables such as wealth and occupational status. The evidence on mean age at death has been derived from three sources: the reconstitution data, the probate records (Essex County Probate Docket, Essex County Probate Court, Salem, Massachusetts), and the vital records of Beverly and Wenham. I linked together the probate records and the vital records, obtaining known ages at death for 51 percent of the decedents in Beverly and 53 percent in Wenham. The distribution of known deaths among decedents increased over time:

Known Deaths among All Decedents

	1681–1720	*1721–1760*	*1761–1800*	*1801–1840*	*N*
Beverly	23%	44%	51%	59%	(688)
Wenham	28%	53%	43%	74%	(109)

The distribution of ages at death by time period, however, reveals that the data after 1720 are more consistent. Still, more men died at younger ages in Beverly between 1801 and 1840, as this table illustrates:

Age	*1681–1720*	*1721–1760*	*1761–1800*	*1801–1840*	*Total*
20–39					
Beverly	18%	19%	16%	28%	23%
Wenham	33%	13%	12%	16%	15%
40–59					
Beverly	27%	37%	34%	25%	29%
Wenham	17%	26%	20%	27%	24%
60+					
Beverly	55%	45%	50%	47%	48%
Wenham	50%	61%	68%	57%	60%
Total N					
Beverly	(22)	(96)	(147)	(287)	(552)
Wenham	(6)	(23)	(25)	(37)	(91)

The chi square value for Beverly was 0.0497; for Wenham, it was 0.8741.

Clearly, the quantity and strength of the evidence from Beverly surpasses that of Wenham. Still, the Wenham data does yield patterns that are of utility.

14. Although the differences in mean ages at death among matured sons, migrants, and nonmigrants were not statistically significant, I am reporting these findings because of the need to begin to gather data on migrant groups in early America.

15. Also, see Chapter six for a discussion of mean age at death and occupational status.

16. Deaths of maritime-related occupations were calculated from "A List of Deaths in Beverly Made by Col. Robert Hale," *Essex Institute Historical Collections,* 5 (1863), 22–24. The crude death rate (deaths per 1000 persons) in 1741 was 20.3; in 1750–1751, it was 19.1. The overall crude death rate for the years 1732–1764 ranged between 20.0 and 25.7.

17. Although I have presented the mean ages at death of women based on the reconstitution data, the numbers were so small that the conclusions must remain speculative. The Beverly data suggest an increase in mean ages at death for women during the eighteenth century. The Wenham evidence conforms to this trend, but the number is too small to suggest a firm pattern. Among female decedents, who comprised between 16 and 20 percent of those with estates probated, almost two-thirds of those in Beverly died over the age of sixty, and 14 percent died under the age of thirty-nine. This same pattern occurred in Wenham.

18. When controlling occupational status by age at death in Beverly for decedents who died 1761–1800, we have the following results:

		Beverly	
Occupation	*20–39*	*40–59*	*60+*
Gentlemen	3%	8%	16%
Professions	3%	2%	2%
Traders	—	8%	—
Mariners	50%	23%	10%
Artisans	17%	29%	12%
Farmers	7%	23%	36%
Women	20%	6%	25%
Total N	(30)	(48)	(95)

Chi square significant below the 0.000 level.

The same table for Wenham included only twenty-five decedents and eighteen of them died over the age of sixty years. Most were either gentlemen or farmers.

3. POPULATION TURNOVER AND ECONOMIC PROSPECTS

1. See in particular the work of Kenneth A. Lockridge, "Land, Population, and the Evolution of New England Society 1630–1790," *Past and Present,* 39 (1968), 62–80; "Afterthought, 1970," in Stanley N. Katz, ed., *Colonial America: Essays in Politics and Social Development* (Boston: Little, Brown and Co., 1971), 485–91; and *A New England Town: The First Hundred Years* (New York: W. W. Norton and Co., 1970). The land pressure thesis has been supported by Philip J. Greven, Jr., *Four Generations: Population, Land and Family in Colonial Andover, Massachusetts* (Ithaca: Cornell University Press, 1970); and Robert A. Gross, *The Minutemen and Their World* (New York: Hill and Wang, 1976).

2. I am thinking here of the historians of social mobility and urban life, such as Stephan Thernstrom, *The Other Bostonians: Poverty and Progress in the American Metropolis, 1880–1970* (Cambridge, Mass.: Harvard University Press, 1973); Michael B. Katz, *The People of Hamilton, Canada West* (Cambridge, Mass.: Harvard University Press, 1975); and Elizabeth Hafkin Pleck, *Black Migration and Poverty: Boston, 1865–1900* (New York: Academic Press, 1979). Perhaps the most useful recent sociological study of migrants is Peter M. Blau and Otis Dudley Duncan, *The American Occupational Structure* (New York: John Wiley and Sons, 1967). The conclusions about nineteenth- and twentieth-century America are drawn from these studies, but I want to acknowledge particular indebtedness to Thernstrom, *The Other Bostonians.*

3. Joseph Thompson Dodge, *Genealogy of the Dodge Family of Essex County, Massachusetts, 1629–1894* (Madison: Democrat Printing Co., 1897), I, 56–57.

4. Sidney Goldstein, *Patterns of Mobility 1910–1950: The Norristown Study* (Philadelphia: University of Pennsylvania Press, 1958), 198–203.

5. Ibid., 218–22.

6. Much of the following discussion has been drawn from two of my earlier essays on the topic. See Douglas Lamar Jones, "The Strolling Poor: Transiency in Eighteenth-Century Massachusetts," *Journal of Social History,* 8 (1975), 28–54; and ibid., "Poverty and Vagabondage: The Process of Survival in Eighteenth-Century Massachusetts,"

The New England Historical and Genealogical Register, 133 (1979), 243–54.

7. These conclusions are based on an analysis of 3,362 transient heads of households in Essex County between 1730 and 1789. "Transients," in this sense, are defined as persons "warned out" of the towns of Essex County. Newcomers who were perceived as either economic or societal threats to the towns were formally requested to leave a town by the constable and selectmen. The selectman notified the Essex County Court of General Sessions of the Peace, which had jurisdiction over the warning out procedure. For a fuller description of this procedure, see Jones, "The Strolling Poor."

8. The warning out records in Essex County do not include the ages of the transients. In other towns, at least 15 percent of all transients were "aged"; see John P. Demos, "Old Age in Early New England," in Michael Gordon, ed., *The American Family in Social-Historical Perspective,* 2nd ed. (New York: St. Martin's Press, 1978), 224–31. Transients in eighteenth-century Providence, Rhode Island, were predominantly young, with only 9 percent over the age of fifty; see Lynne E. Withey, "Undesirable Inhabitants: The Transient Poor of Providence, Rhode Island, 1680–1800," (paper presented to the Annual Meeting of the Organization of American Historians, April 1978).

9. On distances that transients migrated, see Jones, "The Strolling Poor"; and Allan Kulikoff, "The Progress of Inequality in Revolutionary Boston," *William and Mary Quarterly,* 28 (1971), 375–412.

10. Computed from Beverly reconstitution data and Eben Putnam, "Soldiers in the French War from Essex County, 1755–1761," *Essex Institute Historical Collections,* 29 (1892), 169–76.

11. See Jones, "The Strolling Poor," which compares the occupational status of transients in Salem in 1791 to the overall occupational structure of Boston in 1790.

12. On English "tramping," see E. J. Hobsbawm, *Laboring Men: Studies in the History of Labor* (New York: Basic Books, Inc., 1967), 41–74. The Tudor and Stuart background of vagabondage in England is discussed by John Pound, *Poverty and Vagrancy in Tudor England* (London: Harlow, Longman, 1971). For a comparison of the changes in the laws affecting vagrants in England and America, see William J. Chambliss, "A Sociological Analysis of the Law of Vagrancy," *Social Problems,* 12 (1964), 67–77. Chambliss argues that American vagrancy (i.e. transiency) laws were merely adaptations of their English counterparts. He fails to take into account the fact that Massachusetts

laws were specific responses to social change within the American experience. Increased regulation occurred in both England and America, but criminal sanctions against transients were more common in England than in Massachusetts.

13. In Boston, 28 percent of the transients warned in 1791 by the Overseers of the Poor were from foreign countries; 71 percent arrived from towns within Massachusetts. Boston figures apply to the total population of transients, rather than households; see Kulikoff, "The Progress of Inequality in Revolutionary Boston," 400–401, Table X. Of the Salem transients who entered from within Massachusetts, 57 percent were from within ten miles. Forty-six percent of the domestic transients to Boston were from within ten miles.

14. Distances calculated from "Salem Warnings, 1791," *Essex Institute Historical Collections,* 43 (1907), 345–52.

15. *Wenham Town Records, 1730–1775* (Salem: Newcomb and Gauss, 1940), 40.

16. William Vannan's movements were traced from "Nathaniel Hubbard Dodge—His Book, Anno Dom, 1762," the family account book used by Jacob Dodge, Sr.; Wenham Case, 1763, Record Book of the Essex County Court of General Sessions of the Peace, Salem, Massachusetts; and Wenham reconstitution data. The Dodge account book is in the Wenham Historical Association and Museum, Inc., Wenham, Massachusetts.

4. ECONOMIC MOBILITY

1. This description of Jacob Dodge and his family is taken from the following sources: "Nathaniel Hubbard Dodge—His Book, Anno Dom, 1762"; Joseph Thompson Dodge, *Genealogy of the Dodge Family of Essex County, Massachusetts, 1629–1894,* (Madison: Democrat Printing Co., 1894), I, 73–74; 120–21; and *passim;* and *Wenham Town Records, 1776–1810* (Salem: Newcomb and Gauss, 1959). I have also relied on the Wenham tax lists and reconstitution data.

2. The classic study of social mobility in modern America is Peter M. Blau and Otis Dudley Duncan, *The American Occupational Structure* (New York: John Wiley and Sons, 1967); also, see Seymour Martin Lipset and Reinhard Bendix, *Social Mobility in Industrial Society* (Berkeley: University of California Press, 1959). The historical studies of social and economic mobility are extensive, but the most important include Stephan Thernstrom, *The Other Bostonians: Poverty and Progress in the American Metropolis, 1880–1970* (Cambridge,

Mass.: Harvard University Press, 1973), and Michael B. Katz, *The People of Hamilton, Canada West* (Cambridge, Mass.: Harvard University Press, 1975).

3. The distinction between migrants and nonmigrants, common to the studies of nineteenth- and twentieth-century population turnover, rarely appears in the literature on colonial America. One of the most useful studies in this regard was Philip Greven, Jr.'s *Four Generations: Population, Land, and Family in Colonial Andover, Massachusetts* (Ithaca: Cornell University Press, 1970), who defined the idea of "maturing sons." More recently, a study of seventeenth-century Windsor, Connecticut, distinguished between migrants and nonmigrants; see Linda Auwers Bissell, "From One Generation to Another: Mobility in Seventeenth-Century Windsor, Connecticut," *William and Mary Quarterly,* 31 (1974), 79–110. Maris Vinovskis, "American Historical Demography: A Review Essay," *Historical Methods Newsletter,* 4 (1971), 141–48, raises important methodological questions about Greven's *use* of the concept of maturing sons; however, the idea of maturing or native sons remains an important one.

4. At this point in our analysis, we will shift from a focus on the cohorts of taxpayers by decade and collapse all of the tax lists into one. This methodology permits us to retrieve more information about various groups of migrants and nonmigrants for Beverly and Wenham.

5. On Concord, see Robert A. Gross, *The Minutemen and Their World* (New York: Hill and Wang, 1976), 207–9, fn. 16. The evidence for Hingham is presented in Daniel Scott Smith, "Population, Family, and Society in Hingham, Massachusetts, 1635–1880," (unpublished Ph.D. dissertation, University of California, Berkeley, 1973), 112–15; 199, Appendix III–17. While the conclusions of these studies support those described for Beverly and Wenham, the precise measures of intragenerational mobility, as well as the time periods covered, were generally not identical. Also, the Concord and Hingham evidence has not been analyzed according to migrant status.

6. For the Boston evidence, see Allan Kulikoff, "The Progress of Inequality in Revolutionary Boston," *William and Mary Quarterly,* 28 (1971), 404–8.

5. FAMILY FORMATION AND MIGRATION

1. On coming of age in colonial Massachusetts, see John Demos, *A Little Commonwealth: Family Life in Plymouth Colony* (New York: Oxford University Press, 1970), 150–70; Michael Zuckerman, *Peace-*

able Kingdoms: New England Towns in the Eighteenth Century (New York: Alfred A. Knopf, 1970), 72–84; and, for a slightly later time period, Joseph A. Kett, *Rites of Passage: Adolescence in America, 1790 to the Present,* (New York: Basic Books, 1977), 11–37. On the ideals of marriage, see Edmund S. Morgan, *The Puritan Family: Religion and Domestic Relations in Seventeenth-Century New England,* rev'd and enl., (New York: Harper and Row, 1966), 29–64.

2. The precise dating of the changes in ages at first marriage is complicated by the fact that historians have employed different definitions of both the birth and the marriage cohort. In Table 5–1, I have summarized the recent findings divided by both birth and marriage cohorts.

3. The standard analysis of the sex ratio of immigrants to New England is by Herbert Moller, "Sex Composition and Correlated Culture Patterns of Colonial America," *William and Mary Quarterly,* 2 (1945), 116–17. However, he did not control for the marital status of the immigrants. From a sample of passenger lists, the sex ratio (males to 100 females) of single persons who immigrated to New England during the early seventeenth century was 333, almost twice as high as his estimates. Sex ratio of single persons calculated from Nathaniel Bradstreet Shurtleff, M.D., "The Passengers of the Mayflower in 1620," *The New England Historical and Genealogical Register,* 1 (1847), 47–53; Eben Putnam, "Two Early Passenger Lists, 1635–1637," ibid., 124 (1921), 217–26; "More Passengers for New England," looseleaf insert in Samuel G. Drake, *Result of Some Researches Among the British Archives for Information Relative to the Founders of New England* (Boston: The New England Historical and Genealogical Register, 1860); John Camden Hotten, ed., *The Original Lists of Persons of Quality . . . and Others who Went from Great Britain to the American Plantations, 1600–1700* (New York: G. A. Baker, 1931), 42; 44; 277–79; 280–82; 289–92; 293–95; 298–300; Charles Boardman, ed., "Transcript of Three Registers of Passengers from Great Yarmouth to Holland and New England, 1637–1639," *Norfolk Record Society,* 25 (1954), xxv. No passenger lists were used twice in these calculations, although several versions of the same list were examined.

4. See J. Hajnal, "European Marriage Patterns in Perspective," in D. V. Glass and D. E. C. Eversley, eds., *Population in History: Essays in Historical Demography* (London: E. Arnold, 1965), 101–43. The

mean age at first marriage for men in preindustrial England was at least twenty-six to twenty-eight years. More recent evidence of high ages at first marriage in pre-1750 English villages may be found in David Levine, *Family Formation in an Age of Nascent Capitalism* (New York: Academic Press, 1977), 61–66; 97; 113; 123.

5. To compare the mean ages at marriage of men by birth cohorts in Beverly and Wenham, combined F-tests and t-tests as well as simple t-tests were used. The combination of F-tests and t-tests is appropriate if there are significant statistical differences between three or more groups of means (in this case, mean ages at first marriage), while t-tests alone are used to compare pairs of groups. Once a significant relationship was established to exist among the birth cohorts, through the use of the F-test and a standard of judgment below the 0.05 level of significance, t-tests were used to examine the differences between each pair of cohorts. In sum, the F-test establishes the significance of the differences among all of the mean ages in the different birth cohorts; the t-tests permit comparisons among birth cohorts. The findings from these tests are reported below:

(a) The F-test for the birth cohorts of males at age of first marriage in Beverly was significant at 0.268, with an ETA equal to 0.014. This means that the variation among the Beverly birth cohorts on the mean age at marriage of males had not occurred by chance alone. Thus, we must reject the conclusion that variation in age at marriage in Beverly occurred as a result of change over time, from one cohort to another. The ETA represents the amount of the variance explained by the difference among the birth cohorts, which in Beverly was very low, only about 1 percent. Since the F-test is not statistically significant, it is not legitimate to expect to find (nor did I find) differences within the different birth cohorts which were statistically significant with the t-tests.

(b) For Wenham, the F-test was highly significant, at 0.005, with an ETA of 0.097. The differences among the birth cohorts of men at age of first marriage in Wenham did not arise from chance, and, moreover, almost 10 percent of the variance is accounted for by differences in birth cohorts.

The t-tests for Wenham reveal more clearly this strong declining mean age at marriage from 1661 to 1760. The birth cohorts before 1700 revealed consistent statistical differences with those cohorts born after 1700. The greatest contrasts were between the 1661–1680 cohort and the 1741–1760 cohort, in which 26 percent of the variance was explained by differences between the two cohorts, significant at the 0.002 level. Generally, the cohort 1661–1680 was compared with the later cohorts as follows: 1701–1720, significant under the 0.05 level, variance at 8 percent; 1721–1740, significant at 0.005, variance at 13 percent; 1741–1760, significant at 0.002, variance at 26 percent. The cohort 1681–1700 compared as follows: 1701–1720, significant at 0.199, variance at 2 percent; 1721–1740, significant under 0.05, variance at 6 percent; 1741–1760, significant under 0.05, variance at 12 percent. The t-tests between birth cohorts during the eighteenth century were not significant under the 0.05 level.

(c) An additional note: F-tests on Beverly and Wenham males by marriage cohorts were not significant below the 0.05 level, although an occasional t-test was significant. The latter clustered around the period 1721–1740 in Wenham, when population pressure was great. Also, F-tests for women in Beverly and Wenham by birth and marriage cohorts did not reveal significant results.

6. The marital status of matured sons at their first appearance on a tax list in Beverly and Wenham was as follows:

Year and Town	*Married before*	*Married after*	*Unmarried*	*Unknown*	*N*
1731					
Beverly	n.a.	n.a.	n.a.	n.a.	n.a.
Wenham	67%	33%	—	—	(9)
1741					
Beverly	47%	37%	11%	5%	(62)
Wenham	93%	7%	—	—	(14)
1751					
Beverly	67%	21%	6%	6%	(63)
Wenham	74%	26%	—	—	(19)
1761					
Beverly	64%	25%	4%	7%	(75)
Wenham	65%	30%	4%	—	(23)
1771					
Beverly	66%	28%	4%	4%	(87)
Wenham	78%	22%	—	—	(18)
Total					
Beverly	61%	28%	6%	6%	(287)
Wenham	75%	24%	1%	—	(83)

The evidence in this table is taken from the Beverly and Wenham tax lists and reconstitution data.

7. Salem v. Andover, 3 *Mass.* 436 (1807).

8. Calculated by the author from Joseph B. Felt, "Statistics of Population in Massachusetts," *Collections of the American Statistical Association,* I, Part II (Boston, 1845), 149.

9. Diary of Mary Orne Tucker, Haverhill, Massachusetts, May 12, 1802. Located in the Essex Institute, Salem, Mass. I am indebted to Nancy Cott for this reference.

10. The number of widows in Beverly between 1734 and 1737 ranged between fifty-one and sixty. In 1748, there were sixty-three widows and only nine widowers. Taken from "Hale Memoranda," *Essex Institute Historical Collections,* 5 (1863), 280–81. More generally, consult Alexander Keyssar, "Widowhood in Eighteenth-Century Massachusetts: A Problem in the History of the Family," *Perspectives in American History,* 7 (1974), 83–119.

11. Taken from Joseph Thompson Dodge, *Genealogy of the Dodge Family of Essex County, Massachusetts, 1629–1894* (Madison: Democrat Printing Co., 1894), 70–71. For a discussion of the limitations of marital migration as an indicator of mobility, see W. R. Catton and R. J. Smircich, "Propinquity in Mate Selection Reassessed," in Michael Anderson, ed., *Sociology of the Family: Selected Readings* (Middlesex: Harmondsworth, Penguin, 1971), 186–99.

12. Other studies of marital migration in Massachusetts include Alan C. Swedlund, "The Genetic Structure of an Historical Population: A Study of Marriage and Fertility in Old Deerfield, Massachusetts," *Research Reports,* No. 7, Department of Anthropology, University of Massachusetts, Amherst, Mass. (May 1971); Susan L. Norton, "Marital Migration in Essex County, Massachusetts, in the Colonial and Early Federal Periods," *Journal of Marriage and the Family,* 35 (1973) 406–18; and Philip J. Greven, Jr., *Four Generations: Population, Land, and Family in Colonial Andover, Massachusetts* (Ithaca: Cornell University Press, 1970), 210–11. Two more recent studies are Doris O'Keefe, "Marriage and Migration in Colonial New England: A Study in Historical Population Geography," *Discussion Paper Series,* No. 16, Department of Geography, Syracuse University, Syracuse, N.Y. (June 1976); and Cathy Kelly, "Marriage Migration in Massachusetts, 1765–1790," *Discussion Paper Series,* No. 30, Department of Geography, Syracuse University, Syracuse, N.Y. (March 1977).

13. The following discussion of marital migration in Beverly and Wenham is drawn from a sample of the *Vital Records of Beverly,*

Massachusetts to the End of the Year 1849 (Salem: Newcomb and Gauss, 1907), II, and the *Vital Records of Wenham, Massachusetts to the End of the Year 1849* (Salem: Newcomb and Gauss, 1904). The marriages listed in the vital records usually contain the names of the spouses, residential origins at marriage, the dates of the marriages, and whether an "intention" to marry was filed. The vital records do not distinguish between first and later marriages. In order to control for missing information, the following rules were used to collect the sample: (1) "marriages" only were used, while "intentions" were omitted; (2) distinctions between first and later marriages were not taken into account; (3) in order to prevent duplication of marriages which were sampled (since the marriages are listed under both the husband's and the wife's names), only marriages listed under the husband's name were taken; (4) information on residence either entered in brackets or listed as "formerly of" a certain town was omitted; (5) for Wenham, every other marriage that conformed to the above criteria was taken, whereas in Beverly one in every four marriages was selected.

14. This endogamous pattern in eighteenth-century Beverly also occurred in preindustrial England and France; see Solvi Sogner, "Aspects of the Demographic Situation in Seventeen Parishes in Shropshire 1711–60. An Exercise Based on Parish Registers," *Population Studies,* 17 (1963), 132–33; Charles Tilly, *The Vendée: A Sociological Analysis of the Counterrevolution of 1793* (Cambridge, Mass.: Harvard University Press, 1959).

15. Norton, "Marital Migration in Essex County," 411, provides a useful discussion of the importance of population size. The implications of distance and geographic location in mate selection generally are discussed by Catton and Smircich, "Propinquity in Mate Selection Reassessed."

16. Nonresident marriage patterns in Shropshire, England, showed the same intensely localistic pattern during the eighteenth century; see Sogner, "Aspects of the Demographic Situation in Seventeen Parishes in Shropshire," 132–33.

17. The impact of differential migration on marital patterns in Beverly and Wenham became even more pronounced during the twentieth century. In 1921–1925, rates of marital endogamy in Beverly were 53 percent while in Wenham they were only 15 percent. Thirty years later, in 1951–1955, Beverly's marital endogamy rate declined to 40 percent, while Wenham's fell still lower to 12 percent. The twen-

tieth-century rates of marital endogamy were calculated from the *Annual Report of the Vital Statistics of Massachusetts . . . 1921–25; 1951–55 . . .* (Commonwealth of Massachusetts).

6. INHERITANCE

1. The importance of inheritance has been discussed by Philip J. Greven, Jr., *Four Generations: Population, Land, and Family in Colonial Andover, Massachusetts* (Ithaca: Cornell University Press, 1970); John Demos, *A Little Commonwealth: Family Life in Plymouth Colony* (New York: Oxford University Press, 1970); and Robert A. Gross, *The Minutemen and Their World* (New York: Hill and Wang, 1976). Two of the most innovative analyses of inheritance patterns and intergenerational relations in early New England may be found in Daniel Scott Smith, "Population, Family and Society in Hingham, Massachusetts, 1635–1880," (unpublished Ph.D. dissertation, University of California, Berkeley, 1973); and James A. Henretta, "Families and Farms: *Mentalité* in Pre-Industrial America," *William and Mary Quarterly,* 35 (1978), 3–32.

2. Josiah Batchellor, Jr., to Josiah Batchellor, III, October 31, 1769, in Josiah Batchelder [sic], Documents, Private Papers, 1764–1798, Beverly Historical Society, Beverly, Massachusetts.

3. Josiah Batchelder, Jr., "Crew List of Schooner Dolphin, bound from Beverly to Virginia, 1764," Essex Institute, Salem, Massachusetts.

4. More generally, see Lawrence W. Towner, "A Good Master Well Served: A Social History of Servitude in Massachusetts, 1620–1750," (unpublished Ph.D. dissertation, Northwestern University, 1955).

5. The data in this chapter are drawn primarily from the Essex County Probate Docket, a sixteen-volume index to the estates of those persons who were examined by the probate court. All adults who appeared in Beverly and Wenham before 1840 were used to complete the analysis.

6. On Andover, see Greven, *Four Generations,* 125–72; and for Salem, see Paul Boyer and Stephen Nissenbaum, *Salem Possessed: The Social Origins of Witchcraft* (Cambridge, Mass.: Harvard University Press, 1974), 80–109. The seventeenth-century history of land pressure has been most recently analyzed by David Thomas Konig, *Law and Society in Puritan Massachusetts, Essex County, 1629–1692* (Chapel Hill: University of North Carolina Press, 1979), 35–63.

7. John Winthrop, *Winthrop's Journal, 1630–1649,* ed. by James

Kendall Hosmer (New York: Charles Scribner's Sons, 1908), II, 263.

8. Myron O. Allen, *The History of Wenham* (Boston: Bazin and Chandler, 1860), 49–53; and Edwin M. Stone, *History of Beverly* (Boston: James Muroe and Co., 1843), 191–92.

9. *Wenham Town Records, 1707–1731* (Topsfield: The Perkins Press, 1938), 9–150.

10. See petition dated November 27, 1729, *Journal of the House of Representatives of Massachusetts,* 9, 1729–31; *Wenham Town Records, 1730–1775* (Salem: Newcomb and Gauss, 1940), 25.

11. Daniel Scott Smith, "Underregistration and Bias in Probate Records: An Analysis of Data from Eighteenth-Century Hingham, Massachusetts," *William and Mary Quarterly,* 32 (1975), 100–110. Smith finds that 36 percent of the men from Hingham left wills, a figure comparable to that in Beverly but lower than that in Wenham.

12. This distinction between passing on "social status" and "property" is made by E. P. Thompson, "The Grid of Inheritance: A Comment," in Jack Goody et al., eds., *Family and Inheritance: Rural Society in Western Europe, 1200–1800* (Cambridge, England: Cambridge University Press, 1976), 328–60.

13. George L. Haskins, *Law and Authority in Early Massachusetts* (New York: Macmillan, 1960), 171–72; also see his more detailed discussion in "The Beginning of Partible Inheritance in the American Colonies," *Yale Law Journal,* 101 (1941–1942), 1280–1315.

14. Charles McLean Andrews, "The Influence of Colonial Conditions as Illustrated in the Connecticut Intestacy Law," in David H. Flaherty, ed., *Essays in the History of Early American Law* (Chapel Hill: University of North Carolina Press, 1969), 336–66.

15. William E. Nelson, *Americanization of the Common Law* (Cambridge, Mass.: Harvard University Press, 1975), 48. Nelson is one of the first legal historians to recognize the need for a detailed analysis of colonial wills.

16. Richard B. Morris, *Studies in the History of Early American Law* (New York: Columbia University Press, 1930), 82, discusses the Maine wills; for Andover, see Greven, *Four Generations,* 222–58.

17. Estate of Nathaniel Goodhew, 1723, Essex County Probate Records, Book 15, 4–6, Essex County Registry of Probate, Salem, Massachusetts. Robert A. Gross also identified this concept of not "spoiling the whole" in his essay on "The Problem of Agricultural Crisis in Eighteenth-Century New England: Concord, Massachusetts,

as a Test Case," paper presented at the 90th Annual Meeting of the American Historical Association, 1975. Also, see Henretta, "*Mentalité* in Pre-Industrial America," 27–28.

18. Estate of Issac Ellwell, 1723, Essex County Probate Records, Book 15, 47–49.

7. CONCLUSION

1. Frederick Jackson Turner, *The Frontier in American History* (New York: Henry Holt and Co., 1920); Ray Allen Billington, *The Far Western Frontier, 1830–1860* (New York: Harper, 1956); Richard Hofstadter and Seymour Martin Lipset, eds., *Turner and the Sociology of the Frontier* (New York: Basic Books, 1968).

2. Oscar Handlin, *Boston's Immigrants* (Cambridge, Mass.: Harvard University Press, 1959); Stephan Thernstrom, *The Other Bostonians: Poverty and Progress in the American Metropolis, 1880–1970* (Cambridge, Mass.: Harvard University Press, 1973); Michael B. Katz, *The People of Hamilton, Canada West* (Cambridge, Mass.: Harvard University Press, 1975).

3. An important synthesis of such studies—including an analysis of migration—is being completed by David Hackett Fischer.

4. In determining trends in geographic mobility, in- and out-migration statistics are the most useful because they take into account mortality. But because source materials are often sparse and normally underrecorded, complete measurement of the extent of migration in a wide number of colonial towns becomes problematic. Also, it is useful if the lists of inhabitants which are compared over time reflect similar recording procedures. This is nearly an impossible task, as governmental changes altered the requirements for listing inhabitants. Before 1790, tax and valuation lists provided the most consistent nominal listings of male inhabitants in New England towns. Most females and some maturing sons were excluded from these lists, although some women were taxed. However, the fact remains that there were no consistent listings of women as there are of men. After 1790, the U.S. Census enumerated male and female residents in most towns and cities. Recording procedures in the census varied from community to community, however. As defined here, persistence rates include persons, primarily males, who appeared on consecutive lists at regularized time intervals. The ten-year period was chosen to permit comparisons with persistence rates calculated from census materials. Persistence rates

enable us to understand the extent of residential permanence, and by implication, discontinuity.

5. John Demos, "Notes on Life in Plymouth Colony," *William and Mary Quarterly,* 22 (1965), 264–86. For descriptions of the process of migration to open lands, see Sumner Chilton Powell, *Puritan Village: The Formation of a New England Town* (Middletown: Wesleyan University Press, 1963); Philip J. Greven, Jr., *Four Generations: Population, Land, and Family in Colonial Andover, Massachusetts* (Ithaca: Cornell University Press, 1970); Edward S. Perzel, "Landholding in Ipswich," *Essex Institute Historical Collections,* 104 (1968), 302–28.

6. For example, a small group of residents of Wenham, Massachusetts, migrated to Chelmsford in 1656. Chelmsford was a small community with a sizeable land grant, but it needed a minister. Wenham's minister was quite anxious to relocate in Chelmsford and apparently convinced several families to relocate with him. After some disagreement over the terms under which the minister would settle, the Wenham group finally migrated to Chelmsford. See Diary of John Fiske, 1637–1675, (typescript copy), 177–80, in Essex Institute, Salem, Mass.; and William Waters, *History of Chelmsford, Massachusetts* (Lowell: Courier-Citizen Co., 1917), 9–12. More generally, see T. H. Breen and Stephen Foster, "Moving to the New World: The Character of Early Massachusetts Immigration," *William and Mary Quarterly,* 30 (1973), 189–222.

7. In 1800, the crude birth rate in the United States was 55.0 per 1000 white women; in 1850, it was 43.3; in 1900, it was 31.5; and in 1950, it was 23.0. See *Historical Statistics of the United States, Colonial Times to 1957* (Washington, D.C.: Government Printing Office, 1961), 23. The completed family size from five separate studies of pre-1800 America and Canada was 7.6 persons. The average number of children per wife in six studies was 6.3 persons. See Robert V. Wells, "Quaker Marriage Patterns in a Colonial Perspective," *William and Mary Quarterly,* 29 (1972), 438, Table IX.

8. The index of settlement formation illustrated in Figures 7–2 and 7–3 was compiled from Kevin H. White, *Historical Data Relating to Counties, Cities, and Towns in Massachusetts* (Commonwealth of Massachusetts, 1966). Because this index is limited to towns within the boundaries of modern Massachusetts, New Hampshire and Maine were excluded. It employs the initial dates of settlement formation which

were based on the dates of "founding," not the dates of political recognition. In order to generate the most useful and accurate series of population dispersion, the earliest date of settlement formation was used, particularly of districts and plantations.

9. On the powers of towns, districts, and plantations, see *Mass. Acts and Resolves,* I (1662–1714), ch. 10, 505–6; and John Fairfield Sly, *Town Government in Massachusetts (1620–1930)* (Cambridge, Mass.: Harvard University Press, 1930).

10. *Mass. Acts and Resolves,* IV (1757–68), ch. 1, fn at 5; ch. 12, 468; ibid., V (1769–80), ch. 3, 419–20.

11. In 1765, 114 settlements in the eastern counties contained 81 percent of the population; the remainder (excluding Maine and New Hampshire) lived in 74 settlements in the west. In 1800, 138 eastern towns held 61 percent of the white population, while 279 western settlements had grown to include 39 percent. But by 1830, the eastern counties contained 72 percent of the population. Population figures are from Joseph B. Felt, "Statistics of the Population in Massachusetts," *Collections of the American Statistical Association,* I, Part II (Boston, 1845), 148–55 U.S. Bureau of the Census, *Second Census* (Washington, D.C., 1800), 8–12; 13–14; U.S. Bureau of the Census, *Fifth Census* (Washington, D.C., 1830), 16–21. This dispersion of the population in 1800 is also discussed by Jesse Chickering, *A Statistical View of the Population of Massachusetts* (Boston: C. C. Little and J. Brown, 1846).

12. Perry Miller, *The New England Mind: From Colony to Province* (Cambridge, Mass.: Harvard University Press, 1953). Richard Bushman, *From Puritan to Yankee: Character and the Social Order in Connecticut, 1690–1765* (Cambridge, Mass.: Harvard University Press, 1967); Kenneth A. Lockridge, *A New England Town: The First Hundred Years* (New York: W. W. Norton, 1970).

APPENDIX

1. For a general background to underrecorded vital statistics, see Robert Gutman, "Birth and Death Registration in Massachusetts, I. The Colonial Background, 1639–1800," *The Milbank Memorial Fund Quarterly,* 36 (1958), 58–74; and James H. Cassedy, *Demography in Early America: Beginnings of the Statistical Mind, 1600–1800* (Cambridge, Mass.: Harvard University Press, 1969).

2. Philip J. Greven, Jr., *Four Generations: Population, Land, and*

Family in Colonial Andover, Massachusetts (Ithaca: Cornell University Press, 1970), 4–5. Greven's migration rates are drawn from his four generations, which limit precise comparison with other methods of calculating population turnover.

3. For the methodological discussion of Smith's work, see his "Population, Family and Society in Hingham, Massachusetts, 1635–1880" (unpublished Ph.D. dissertation, University of California, Berkeley, 1973), 19–83. A more accessible example of the fruits of his research may be found in his article, "The Demographic History of Colonial New England," *The Journal of Economic History,* 32 (1972), 165–83.

4. Kenneth A. Lockridge, "The Population of Dedham, Massachusetts, 1636–1736," *Economic History Review,* 19 (1966), 318–44. One of the few methodological critiques of Lockridge's work is W. R. Prest, "Stability and Change in Old and New England: Clayworth and Dedham," *The Journal of Interdisciplinary History,* 6 (1976), 359–74.

5. For example, see Smith, "Demographic History of Colonial New England," as well as his more recent essay, "The Estimates of Early American Historical Demographers: Two Steps Forward, One Step Back, What Steps in the Future?" *Historical Methods,* 12 (1979), 24–38. In addition, consult Maris A. Vinovskis, "Mortality Rates and Trends in Massachusetts before 1860," *The Journal of Economic History,* 32 (1972), 184–213.

6. Stable population theory and model life tables suggest that the mortality levels of adult taxpayers were slightly higher in Beverly and Wenham than the recorded, decennial rates indicate. The adjusted model, based on the Model West Life Tables, Levels 10 and 15, reveal that the proportions of adult deaths for males ages twenty-one to sixty were 20.9 percent for Level 10, and 23.8 percent for Level 15. These mortality rates are based on an intrinsic growth rate of 25/1000, and derived from the percentage of persons under sixteen in Essex County in 1765. Just as the recorded model suggests, there was a range of mortality experiences in New England towns before 1800. See Ansley J. Coale and Paul Demeny, *Regional Model Life Tables and Stable Populations* (Princeton: Princeton University Press, 1966), 140–41; 150–51.

INDEX

LIBRARY OF CONGRESS CATALOGING IN PUBLICATION DATA

Jones, Douglas L.
Village and seaport, migration and society in eighteenth-century Massachusetts.

Bibliography: p.
Includes index.
1. Migration, Internal—Massachusetts—History—18th century. 2. Beverly (Mass.)—Social conditions. 3. Wenham (Mass.)—Social conditions. I. Title.
HB1985.M4J66 304.8'2'097445 80–54469
ISBN 0–87451–200–X AACR2